People

ARE NOT

What you think

a different perspective

KAREEN L. NELSON

Book Cover: Mario Chambers
Graphic Designer Xpress Color – Mario@xpresscolor.com

Barracks Editorial & Design House, LLC –
iambevtheeditor@gmail.com

ISBN-978-0-578-73593-1

Printed in the United States of America

Dedication

In memory of my late mother, Gloria Icilda Coke, for being a lovely expression of God's love. Miss you, my memories of all you have done for me are forever in my heart.

To my husband Eddy. It's not what we have in life, but who we have in our life that matters. Thank you for being you.

Table of Contents

A Different Perspective

Introduction

Have you ever met or looked at someone that you had an intuition about, and later found it to be the truth? We all have had our share of good or suspicious or immediate instinctive feelings about someone we either knew or did not know. Did you understand what you were thinking, or perhaps, you pondered with the idea and then regretted not acting on it? It's when you know something quickly, or you interpret something without relying on your conscious reasoning.

This experience begins with intuition a selective intuitive (in-built guidance) for us to choose over the thought that arises from our mind is what we become. So then, an impression is felt like an idea, an image, a vision, or awareness of knowing something without really being able to explain. Let me say it better; it's a knowing through your thoughts. Maybe, you didn't understand that this goes deeper than just thinking about someone; it's about how a thought connects with us as spiritual beings.

For example, I thought I knew enough about people to pin-point someone's personality after our first conversation. When I discern something about others, society marks me by saying, "you are deep." I never considered myself deep, so where did I get this knowledge? Genesis (the first book of the Bible) states that all knowledge is from God, the Creator of Heaven and Earth.

1

When we acknowledge that only God knows the future because He Created everything, but humankind has a will. God allows us to choose our outcome in life; He already knows our choices and our will to choose.

Intuition is God's prompting through our spirit, unmistakable evidence of the closeness He desires to share in our daily lives. Meaning He understands who we are and still wants to reach out to us because He cares.

For the most part, our thoughts are a gateway to affecting our lives for the better. However, we need to understand who and what influences our thoughts and our role in this experience.

Generally, what we see in others is the effect of an inner cause introduced through thoughts into our minds directly affecting the heart, and then we react based upon our perception. Here's a revelation, all mankind struggles within themselves for either good or evil to dominate us. The fight within us all is for evil to dominate our minds while the enemy tries to direct us away from God.

Some people say, no matter what they do, life is a struggle, and they struggle within to find themselves. I've heard people say, maybe God loves some people, but they don't think He loves them. Perhaps you have said, but if that's true, then why is my life such a mess?

It began in heaven as a thought from a created being who wanted to over throw God and become God. Through his freedom of choice and rebellious nature, he became the self-exalted one; satan. Satan also became God's adversary by introducing the seed of rebellion on earth through a thought when he led Adam and Eve into disobeying God. Being a deceiver, the serpent said to Eve, *"You will not certainly die"* *by eating from the tree of the knowledge of good and evil.* **Paraphrased—Genesis 3:4—KJV.**

Eve reasoned within herself after she believed a false doctrine from the enemy. In fact, by leaving out the truth, satan allowed for doubt to enter into their thoughts so they could exercise their freedom of choice and choose wrongly. Thoughts can be powerful with courage, stamina and the fortitude to succeed. We should never underestimate satan; he is sly, and skillful with a lifetime of experience in dealing with humanity. The most terrible effect of this lie is on the loving relationship between God and humankind. Before this, we only knew what was good. We had good thoughts and an undisputable relationship with God. Now we understand the difference between good and evil and the power to choose.

As a result of their disobedience, Adam granted satan access to deposit negative thoughts into our heads because Adam acted as humanity's representative. This access is the reason why some of our lives are a mess because we have allowed the truth about ourselves to be altered and through our thoughts to manifest. Don't allow the enemy (satan) to change your narrative with a negative mindset; see yourself as beloved of God with the potential to do good.

We can approach God based on what Jesus did for us on the cross, not based on our worthiness. Remember that because the devil doesn't want us to know this.

Though the devil is a powerful foe, we can defeat him by knowing his nature, so we're not ignorant of his plans—to be discussed later.

2 Corinthians 2:11—KJV— *"lest satan should get an advantage of us; for we are not ignorant of his devices."* Satan's knowledge is limited; he is unlike the omnipresent God, so he will never know all of our thoughts.

God is omnipresent; He's all knowing, but satan's knowledge is limited so he can't know all of our thoughts. Because we all have a limited perception about others, it's about seeking the Creator over all things. This is key in navigating through life beyond our five senses; tools that we use to perceive and understand our surroundings. For instance, there were times that God brought people into my life that I would not have chosen as friends based on their looks and personality. It's because, as a human being, I saw through my limited perception. After all, I don't know everything.

We obsess and overvalue our physical appearance because that's how we communicate with other people who we are, but it cannot become a replacement for who we are. Our appearances can change or fade with time, but our character is always with us. Who we present ourselves as, and how we act is more important than our external appearance.

4

There are other characteristics like having a bachelor's degree, being in a higher social class, an attractive personality, good looks, and good self-esteem that can change others' perception of us. We want people to find us likable by capturing their attention in social or private settings in the hope of creating friendships. However, the ultimate goal is to seek friends and colleagues who are authentic.

Authenticity is an essential virtue for all, but still a requirement in people we invite into our lives regardless of physical appearances. It's about being consistent in word and action, being fair and just while being comfortable with your past and yourselves. Generally speaking, we don't like or trust people who come across as phony and untruthful. These two things can be very different; what we perceive people to be and what is truth are not always the same.

Let's Consider This Scenario

You are getting on a bus, but there are only two seats available. One seat is next to a petite, white-haired, elderly woman. The other seat is next to a husky, grim-faced man. Based on your immediate impression, you would sit next to the elderly woman, who turns out to be a skilled pocket picker. You immediately judged the woman as harmless and the man as threatening, leading to the loss of your wallet. Your perception is that an elderly woman could not be a threat. She knew that her appearance would elude you from beholding her truth.

Think about this, when you're out in public, and evaluate a person, you often assess immediately based on age, nationality, color, occupation, or some other traits. This evaluation allows us to make a snap judgment and decision, but it can also lead to a biased or stereotyped perception of other people.

My term for this is called *social categorization* and it is useful at times, but it can also lead to misjudgments as in this situation. Although *social categorization* happens automatically and unconsciously, we cannot truly judge someone through rating. With this in mind, instantly, you will likely see the elderly or anyone you are about to be seated with differently, thus reminding us that people are not always what they seem.

In this, like any case, as believers, our ability to discern will tell us to pass by the elderly woman. Your spirit fully understands the situation, which prompts you not to sit there, thus avoiding the loss of your wallet. Even if you are not a believer, your intuition or God's Spirit will alert you of harm. However, the more sensitive your spirit is to hearing or identifying God and your willingness to obey Him, the more relaxed and fulfilling your life will become.

A Person's True Nature Isn't Always Visible

Matthews 7:15-20.

"Beware of false prophets, who come to you in sheep's clothing, but inwardly they are ravenous wolves. You will know them by their fruits. Do men gather grapes from thorn bushes or figs from thistles? Even so, every good tree bears good fruit, but a bad tree bears bad fruit. A good tree cannot bear bad fruit, nor can a bad tree bear good fruit. Every tree that does not bear good fruit is cut down and thrown into the fire. Therefore, by their fruits you will know them."

Proverbs 23:7.

"For as he thinks in his heart, so is he. "Eat and drink!" he says to you, but his heart is not with you."

People are not what they seem; therefore, marketers and artists count on this to make you see people and things the way they want you to see them. Maybe, we don't want to see them for who they are or, perhaps, the truth seems impossible. You can meet someone, and they tell you anything you want to hear without an ounce of truth. We can give off any perception of ourselves to evoke a better persona of ourselves. We tend to show people what they want to see without it being our truth.

There are many reasons why people are not what you think. An important reason is that we have not received the revelation that our thoughts have transformational powers. It's us rejecting lies, replacing them with the truth about who we are, and then processing those painful memories to bring emotional and spiritual healing.

7

In getting to the root of our struggles, there is a saying called inner healing or the process of becoming more like Jesus. Remember, He is the one who heals the wounded spirit through which painful memories are taken captive and made obedient to Him.

Your identity is in direct correlation to knowing God and having a relationship with Him. He sees you as good and wonderfully made; it's powerful. I will discuss this in a later chapter.

Ironically, we don't share the same energy or drive in developing an intimate relationship with our Creator as we do with people we desire to be close to. The closeness we think or try to have with others may not be authentic by them or us. Instead, we trust others who can quickly leave us hurting, angry, and in complete despair.

We don't trust our Creator, who demonstrated His love for us, in that while we were yet sinners, Christ died for us. **Romans 5:8—paraphrased.**

All you need is a glance into the degree of God's love for you to change your entire outlook on life. Another reason is that people are afraid to be vulnerable. Being vulnerable involves letting yourself feel things, the good, and the bad, and then letting someone else see your nakedness. For instance, we want to think the best of those we think we know. Do we know these people well enough to predict their movements? Are you who everyone thinks you are? **Selah.**

By looking at a person, how can we see their mind and personal thoughts to see their true essence, passions, flaws, or fears? We can't, which is why we settle to judge by their personality, demeanor, attire, or other physical appearances. Why, because we are visual people living by our senses and immediate impressions.

In the natural, physical, or visual realm, people will surprise and outright shock you. They turn out not to be all who we thought they were, and sometimes the clues were right in front of our noses the entire time.

Let's continue this with summarizing some broader views as it relates to impression and truth.

Impressions

We often form impressions of others very quickly, with only minimal information. It's the beginning of the imagination of what you come to expect from each other. For example, when you meet with a new coworker, you immediately begin to develop an initial impression of this person. When you visit the grocery store, you may conclude that the cashier who checks you out is a certain way, even though you know very little about this person.

Admittedly, first impressions are there before you get to know someone or see their flaws.

Consider How Often You Make the Below Judgments Everyday

You ignore one's character because they are pretty, handsome, financially secure, or some other criteria you desire and know is wrong. Be strategic as, during the hiring process of a company, they look carefully at punctuality, communication, judgment, and thoughtfulness.

These four-character traits are commonly reviewed during the interview and those vitally crucial in-between stages. All four-character traits can begin to reveal the real character of a candidate.

Observing an individual's qualities will determine who they are as a person, what's important to them, and if they meet your criteria. It helps to know that people are not perfect, mainly, if you don't expect yourself to be perfect.

You think that you know a person because you share a similar interest, a friendship, a home, or a family. Then one day, it becomes clear that some of your commonality and perspectives are really not the same.

Shall we Examine your Perception?

A person's perception refers to the different mental processes that we use to form impressions of other people. This perception includes not just how we create these impressions, but also the different conclusions we make about other people based on our opinions. Let's take a closer look at how a person's perception works and the impact it has on our day-to-day interactions with other people.

We frequently base our impressions on the roles and social norms we expect from people. Physical clues can also play an important role. If you see a woman dressed in a professional-looking suit, you might immediately assume that she works in a formal setting, perhaps at a law firm or bank. Of course, we tend to focus on the most seeming points rather than noting background information. If you see a woman dressed in a tailored suit and the style of her hair is in a bright pink Mohawk, you are likely to pay more attention to her unusual hairstyle than her business attire.

People often say to me that perception is reality. I think they say this to explain how miscommunication occurred with another person or why they feel the way they do. I am not sure where this phrase originated, but I hear it more lately.

When the truth is concealed by lies or distorted with misinformation, if the perception is reality, humanity is lost. What people perceive is what they believe based on what they hear, see, and think. Mostly we cannot control what happens, but we can always control our reactions and sense of what is right and wrong.

Is Truth Important?

Truth is a universal practice, and it's what we swore to uphold in court and allegedly outside of the courthouse. In the court of law, we must repeat, "I swear to tell the truth, the whole truth, and nothing, but the truth."

Maybe we could make you commit, to tell the truth, if we could get you to associate telling the truth or not lying with some sacred object like the Bible. As we know, most good laws, like the bill of rights and such came from God, which originated in the Ten Commandments.

However, we cover up lies we say every day with the sacred Bible, representing the truth that we don't read or believe. We are not telling the truth, omitting the fact or concealing our hurt and endangering ourselves and others. I think this society has a different perspective when it comes to the truth and their devotion to God. If you love God with all your heart, mind, soul, and spirit, you will love your neighbor (everyone) as yourself.

We are so privy to lies because it is our human nature from after the beginning of creation. Nevertheless, to heal the hurting, we cannot leave out any important information in telling the truth and admitting why we are hurting. Making yourself look better to avoid suspicion or twisting the truth to create a favorable version of something that happened is called a lie.

Truth is critical because it reduces the uncertainty in decision making, creating a favorable outcome. Whereas, not knowing the truth or not having the correct information will cause misunderstanding, fear, hatred, and possibly loss of lives.

My first thoughts about someone I meet for the first time is almost right. Truth be told, you don't want to trust or serve God because He may require you to give up what is ailing you. You may have the desire to, but not deeply enough to make the necessary adjustments.

We are a society inundated with information, but our thoughts and intentions are hidden, making it difficult to predict a person's behavior. The Bible teaches us that God requires our obedience to His laws and His will for our lives to protect us from ourselves, ensuring it will be well with us. However, if we pursue the truth, we will not only find it; we will live in freedom and joy.

What does the Bible say about how Jesus was Perceived by Many?

We know that Jesus is the son of God, the anointed one, but many hated Him because He made the religious people uncomfortable, confused, and angry. It was the religious folks and Jewish people who fueled anger against Christ. They believed that Jesus was a threat to their religious system and to their way of life.

Jesus did not meet their standards of holiness or traditions, which made it impossible for anyone to either observe the sabbath or worship. If we see someone who looks different, speaks differently, or doesn't fit our definition of the 'norm,' we question their validity, and this was their reality with Jesus.

Those who rejected Him didn't want to understand how He did miracles, spoke with authority, and even appeared to be the Messiah. The Jews spoke of the Messiah as a future Jewish king from the Davidic line, who was commissioned by God to save the Jewish nation. They did not believe Jesus to be the Son of God. On that belief, Jews and Christians must continue to differ. Jews believe that all share the divine spirit and stamped with the divine image, and no person, not even the greatest of all people, can possess the perfection of God. No one can be God's equal.

People in those days followed Jesus because He had a heart of compassion; He healed all who came to Him with miracles signs and wonders. Being in His presence transformed lives for the better, so where there were miracles, enormous crowds followed.

Jesus was as the Old Testament scriptures prophesied Him to be. The evidence of Him as the Messiah were many; those who knew Him and those who were eyewitnesses of His life and ministry. Although He was popular, some still did not obey Him nor wanted what He offered. However, for those who did, their lives were forever changed by the power of God.

Ironically, the scribes, Pharisees, and Sadducees, those who supposedly knew scriptures, blamed Him for stirring up trouble. They were likened to religious people today who have a form of godliness, but deny God's power; for those, turn away from. —**Paraphrased—2 Timothy 3:5-KJV.**

We cannot be the religious group of old who knew scriptures but didn't apply it to transform their lives or others. You could say the religious people of old were not what we thought when examining their lifestyle and attitude about Jesus. They knew of God without a relationship with Him.

The Bible is the book of books that bring us to God through Jesus, who is the mediator between God and man. You can read about the life of Jesus and apply your thoughts to knowledge through faith into a true relationship with God.

Needing a Change

If asked, most people would admit to needing a simple lifestyle change. The truth is, everyone has something personal about themselves; they would prefer not to disclose. For example, you may dislike the shape of your nose, middle name, the length of your fingers, weight, or height. Not acknowledging the root cause of your struggle until you do something sinister or live an unfulfilling life.

Perhaps the most damaging is when you tell yourself you can't do that or don't deserve this, which can create a scenario where you imagine yourself to be less than you are through self-images that deny your full potential.

We must allow ourselves not to be okay all of the time. Admit it, this way we don't put pressure on ourselves and live in disgust. Pretending is painful, sad and just hard work. Trying to make everybody like you is equally hard.

We try to avoid the emotional wear down and exhaustion produced by trying not to worry anyone. For the most part, people who feel sad pretend to be alright. Unfortunately, we realize this much too late—pretending to be okay instead of admitting that we are deteriorating within ourselves.

There are many stories about how someone who committed the murder was friendly before committing the act. I've heard this said by numerous people explaining their encounter with a person they just met before a murder. It's too often that we listen to things like the following:

Man shot by driver in passing vehicle;

Man holding girlfriend hostage;

Pursuit ends after crash;

One dead, two others injured in double weekend shoot-ings;

Have you seen her?

Death penalty for man who raped, and murdered girl-friend's daughter;

Police sergeant in custody after deadly shooting.

These examples are a result of us ending up feeling tired of life and devoured by our constant attempts to calm the voice of discomfort from within. It's important to understand, that we are all a mixture of goodness, passion, ignorance and fear. We don't want fear and ignorance to dominate us to live below our potential, nor do we crave passion and goodness only to gratify ourselves.

If you desire to empower others' lives by making a difference in your communities and the world, your passion and goodness must bring glory to God, our Creator. When you hide or deny any of these, you're not honest with yourself or anyone. You're not always right, but you already knew this. Indeed, you have heard something similar said before, or maybe you already knew. It's time to see ourselves as extraordinary visionaries through our thoughts, and as the amazing magnificent spiritual being, we are. Our lives will be free from emotional wear down once we understand the link between our thoughts, feelings, and behavior.

The Power of a Thought

We live in a world full of complicated people. The human brain is the most complicated thing we will ever spend any time thinking about, and we do this in every social interaction. Thinking is what we do all the time. Your mind is rarely blank because practically every moment, you are thinking of something. Even while asleep, you are creating thoughts.

The power of thought is the key that creates your reality. Reality creation is an inside job, and to become the master of your destiny, you must learn to control the natural surroundings of your most powerful or influential thoughts. Your thoughts about yourself will turn into reality.

If you think you are a failure, you will feel like a failure. Then, you will act like a failure, which strengthens your belief that you must be a failure. The assumption that you are a failure makes you feel discouraged and causes you to put in less effort in everything you do.

What you think on long enough you will become, take a moment to think about what you have been thinking. With your commitments and responsibilities, you believe you have little opportunity to develop your inner nature and thoughts. The Bible speaks about the power of the mind and your thoughts to bring you closer to who you are as a spirit being. I think it's easy to glaze over this and overlook the connection between thoughts and transformation.

19

Have you ever thought about what you are thinking, or why do you think the way you do, and what shape your thoughts? Thoughts, for the most part, or rather a collection of thoughts may pop into our head. We should treat thoughts not as simple brain activity, but as powerful forces that may have far-reaching consequences.

Look around you; everything you see is pure thought, able to be moldable, able to influence and be overridden with a more robust thought. It is essential to understand that when a thought enters our mind, we examine it based upon God's Word and determine if we should continue down that path or reject the thought and replace it with another.

Because the mind is powerful, our thoughts shape who we are and will become. What makes us uniquely different is our perception and how we interpret what we take in through our senses. Now, after we have perceived our reality, it is then shaped by how we want it rather than merely the way it is. I will explain our perception and how our thoughts influence every aspect of our existence in a later chapter. I hope to give you facts that will provoke your thought process to seek truth through your thinking and insight into why people are more than our perception because we are great pretenders.

You will become more conscious of your thoughts if you understand how powerful it is to undo your brokenness and bring about your wholeness and happiness. The good news is, you are in charge of your thoughts!

Humans are a remarkable species in that we can do far more with our minds and thought process than any other species. Thoughts are an aloud unspoken concept in our heads before it is a written idea or spoken words out of our mouths. With that said, our thoughts, linked to our emotions, which direct our feelings into our hearts, became our spoken words. Not seriously considering our thoughts has led us to be vulnerable to hate, discouragement, and destructive intentions. The saying, "sticks and stones may break my bones, but words will never hurt me" is not necessarily true. Our words backed by harmful thoughts can hurt a great deal if delivered with intention and focus. They can actually make people mentally and physically sick, but focused thoughts expressed through encouraging words can heal.

Romans 12:2—NLT.

"Don't copy the behavior and customs of this world, but let God transform you into a new person by changing the way you think. Then you will learn to know God's will for you, which is good and pleasing and perfect."

While we can understand what others think, believe, and feel, sometimes we are wrong. We have heard that we should put ourselves in the shoes of others to understand their thoughts and feelings better. However, we need the knowledge that a person already has in his or her head to understand their perspective. For example, say you have a mistaken understanding of another person then no amount of perspective thinking is going to make your judgment accurate. If you want to get that person's perspective, you will need to either be that person or have that person tell you honestly what's on his or her mind. Mistakes like this have wrecked relationships and careers, causing misunderstandings, leading to wrong solutions to society's biggest problems and possible needless wars.

The problem that most of us have is taking in facts, statistics, and information. We don't question the reason behind them or make an effort to analyze what was seen, read, or been taught. The below pie chart is a reflection or overview of mostly our thoughts from non-believers or believers who are not whole, showing the variety of thoughts a person has.

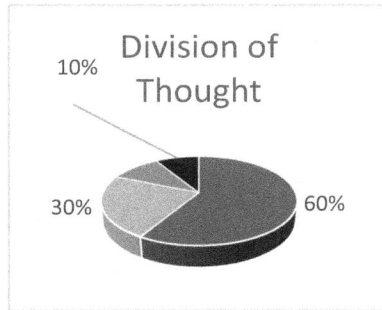

Division of Thought

10%

30%

60%

Shall we say, our problem lies in the whereabouts of our Creator in this chart?

- 10% of thoughts in this model (black) is the amount of time people spent in empathy, that's right 10%. So, you may say people don't care about me. This isn't because people are mean, but simply because they are mostly focused on themselves. 60% of thoughts (dark gray) are self-directed and yeah that's a lot. 30% are directly towards relationship (light gray) and that's also self-directed. Yeah, many of us are consumed with ourselves and our own agenda.

Here are other examples:

- The intention behind our actions are hidden because we don't say really what we think. You say how's your day? The person says, Good, but you were thinking horrible.

- Most behavior is largely selfish.

Many relationships are based on the idea that if I help you, one day, you will help me. We help our close friends and families; as the saying says, blood is thicker than water. People offer aid to boost their self-esteem or reputation. In a transaction, if I purchase a car, both I and the dealer benefit.

- People have trouble remembering things. For example, you receive a text. I'm outside the grocery store, where are you? You say, I'm sorry I really forgot. However, you didn't forget you just did not want to.

- People have stronger feelings about something than they let on. You say to someone you must feel awful. He or she said no, it's not so bad.

He or she is thinking of mental breakdown. It's incredible the people who seem to have it all suffer from bouts of loneliness. There are ordinary people as well with this same problem. Please think about why you feel lonely and why you need to be alone.

Carl Jung said, *"Loneliness doesn't come from having no one around you, but from being unable to communicate the important things that are to you."*

So then, people are too concerned about themselves to give you much attention, they tend to be alone, are more emotional and feel differently than they let on which relates to how someone views their world through thoughts.

Remember, keep your focus on Jesus because He is the author and finisher of your faith. Build up your relationship with God, so when people fail you and they will, you can move on with ease because God is your sustainer and not human-kind. Just trust Him and obey Him; He will bring the right people your way.

Our thoughts cause our Problems

There is no way to reveal the millions of thoughts that you reject, but these often determine your character, the fact that you are not a murderer means you have rejected those thoughts. But why? Why did you reject those thoughts while someone else let them in and believed in them?

One answer is that you sorted your thoughts by fundamental values, by your experiences and gained wisdom and maturity. You sought after love for hate, acceptance for rejection through God's Word, and your relationship with Him. These thoughts then manifest into your story, what you are, and how you behave.

You may not feel you are responsible for your thoughts, and if you are not responsible for how you think, then you do not feel accountable for what happens to you. You will think about yourself as a victim of circumstance, a victim of your thoughts.

Are you really a victim?

Yes, if you think you are!

What if you do not need an occasion to celebrate, but instead, every day is a celebration for you? What if you never fail to give your best in every task? What if you do not want to change anything in yourself or your life? What if you are at peace with your past, fulfilled with your present, and do not worry about your future?

What if you do not find faults with anyone? What if you don't even dread your death? What if you are perpetually happy? What if...? The moment you think that such a state of mind is unachievable, you are trapped. What is the way out of this trap?

Every time you generalize a situation and try to relate it to any of your past experiences, stop yourself. Go back and allow yourself to go through the three steps: assess the situation, derive a conclusion, and then respond.

Give yourself the liberty to go through each situation individually will set you free of the trap. Take your time to analyze and then respond. That is another important thing to remember, always respond to the situation, do not react. Reactions are biased and predictable, whereas; responses are contemplated actions in themselves, free of any strings attached.

Once you are accustomed to this kind of mindset, you will gradually drift away from your perspectives and start functioning independently, with no preconceived notions and presumptions; and that would be your freedom from your trap. It might make you a bit uncomfortable as you no longer refer to previous judgments your mind made for you, but remember, this much discomfort is a process to set yourself free.

For instance, let's say your friend Jim invited you and some of your friends to his house for his birthday party. At the party, an introduction is made with another guest, and immediately, there's a certain comfort level and cohesiveness. You think that person is nice, and you like that person's eye contact. During the conversation, you further perceive that person is a good listener and interacts well with you and others.

About an hour into the conversation, you're laughing, drinking, and having a great time. Two hours have passed, and you feel comfortable to invite that individual to your house for your birthday celebration. However, you are taken back by the response "no" because, that individual is about to break off a relationship, he or she is presently involved in. Wow, why was that person not upfront with you initially, or why did you not inquire if that person was in a relationship?

You were seemingly captivated by that individual's great personality, by their confidence, a flair for style, and an attractive smile. Despite the physical attraction, you were unable to detect the truth hidden on the inside of us all. Our thoughts, those unpleasant experiences we are holding onto, our perspective on life, and so on. In this situation, what have you learned?

Admittedly, you intended to get to know that individual as a friend, romantically, or maybe to be a counselor in that individual's inner self. Whatever your thoughts are, it isn't possible to know anyone by talking or being with them in that length of time.

Thoughts cause most of our problems; they pop into our heads and emerge in the form of words leaving our mouths. This is why people have a hard time observing their thoughts. To overcome your issues, you will need to follow your thoughts rather than continue thinking. You can let your thoughts run amok, but why would you?

It is your mind, your thoughts.

Isn't it time to take your power back?

Isn't it time to take control?

The Bible instructs us to remember (memorize) God's Word. Most actions are conscious, so we will often do what we think. With that in mind, we must understand that what is in us eventually, literally will come out of us. Once the word of God is embedded within you, it will flow from the abundance of your heart to speak life in every situation.

When we memorize God's Word and hide it in our heart **Psalms 119:11** tucked away accessible as needed we are preparing for success. **—Paraphrased.**

We will never do or say what we cannot remember. If you can think it, you will speak life into any dead situation of your life.

Your mind as a Thinker

Have you noticed the quality of your thoughts is directly related to the quality of your daily life? Where your thoughts go, so does your attention. Thinking means concentrating on one thing long enough to develop an idea about it. Not learning other people's opinions, or memorizing a body of information, however, it may sometimes be useful. You are developing your ideas, in short, thinking for yourself.

No skill is more valuable and harder to come by than the ability to think through problems critically. Schools don't teach you a method of thinking. You have to do your due diligence.

I find for myself that my first thought is never my best thought. My first thought is always someone else's; it's still what I've already heard about the subject. It's only by concentrating, sticking to the question, being patient, letting all the parts of my mind come into play that I arrive at my original idea. By giving my brain a chance to make associations, draw connections, and take me by surprise. And often even that idea doesn't turn out to be very good. It would help if you had time to think about it, make mistakes recognize them, make false starts and correct them, and outlast my instincts to defeat my desire to declare the job done and move on to the next thing.

So, it is with any other form of thought. If your thoughts are rotten (self-critical, self-doubting, self-righteous, judgmental), you are likely to feel stuck, unable to connect with your creative possibilities. Nothing will flow for you at that moment, the noticing part is critical; instead decide to do something different. When your thoughts are calm, it is as if your vision opens up, so you're able to see and engage in the situation with greater clarity.

There is a loving voice that creates a feeling of peace and inner harmony. How do you develop a sense of what your voice sounds like when it comes to the most profound experience? Learn to listen to that small quiet voice within you. You'll know it when you hear it because it is loving.

Please get to know it as the voice of truth because that is what it is. It feels completely different in your body than the voices of judgment, doubt, and fear. Most of the world is suffering from a lack of peace from within themselves. You want to stick with positive thoughts to get mostly positive results in life. It's God's Voice of peace-giving us good ideas. Here is where you decipher your experiences, think critically about others, what people say, and their reactions by controlling the nature of your dominant, habitual thoughts.

The conditions and circumstances of your life are as a result of your collective thoughts and beliefs. Think about this when you observe yourself and others, then remember change is accessible through your thought.

Knowing Someone

Most people get stuck as a thinker observer, by rarely interpreting or analyzing what they see. You may think you know a person because you have had conversations with him or her or because you have known them for a while, but do you understand the core of a person?

How well do you know someone, anyone, or maybe that person you were thinking about? Knowing someone is so much more than having facts about them even if it includes the somewhat obscure or out of the ordinary, deeper than recognizing a face.

You only know someone who shares information with you, mainly confidential information. It is necessary to establish a personal bond to get to know what they consider to be important. You can come to know someone by asking them a series of questions and committing their answers to memory until you know them like you know your cell phone number.

But there is something not quite right about knowing someone in that sense, in a manner that mirrors studying or memorizing like a puzzle piece that looks like it should be the one but won't fit. Knowing someone is collecting shared experiences, stumbling upon mannerisms, and their quirks. You anticipate people's reactions to things, knowing when and how their anger will melt. What sparks their passion? What that passion looks like, and what constitutes an expression of their love?

You may often have people who come into your life, claiming to love you and cherish you. While some sincerely do love you, others don't. Although your friends may not know so much about you, it does not necessarily mean they don't care about you. You will be surprised by the answers to a pop quiz about you from your friends and family members. Surprise to hear how little or much they know about your experiences, favorite thing, or general.

Would you be surprised by your answers to a pop quiz about your friends, families, coworkers, neighbors, or acquaintances? We have all been to a party, baby or bridal shower, and a question asked about the honoree you didn't know. You said, "Oh, I didn't know that about them!"

It's because most of the time, we meet up for shared interest meetings/special family gatherings without sharing our hearts. We don't know enough about those we often associate with because we do not share personal information or ask the right questions. Maybe it's easier not to tell because we may have to care, and it's all about me. I know you never said that!

However, you may be surprised to learn that many people do feel like this. Some people are emotionally scarred without the understanding that to forgive and release their hurt is to begin the healing process. If we saw a big heavy iron ball hit someone on their foot, we could imagine what that would be and immediately empathize with the person suffering. When there is pain involved, there's usually a point at which suffering takes place. However, suffering doesn't have to last, but pain can last for days, weeks, or more. And when someone is in pain, we feel empathy because most of us are compassionate people. However, feeling sorry for someone comes from our perception of what suffering is to them. And when you see a homeless person lying on the street, your first thought might be that they're suffering. And you may be right!

But you also may not be right. I recently found out that some homeless people don't want help because they rather live on the streets than deal with life's reality. Sometimes people genuinely suffer, and what appears to be someone suffering is our belief that they are.

You don't know someone's story and you don't know if they are suffering or not until you talk with them. We see a man begging on the street, and automatically we assume he must be hungry, and we are ready to buy him something to eat. What if he needs medication, toothpaste, or a pair of socks?

What if it's a woman standing at the end of the freeway and needs money for baby formula, diapers or shoes? We have no idea what they need unless we ask. If you think about it, such a simple task, if we want to help someone, but many of us don't. Instead, we keep a barrier up and hand that person enough to make ourselves feel better, and then we move on with our lives.

A Different Perspective

We express ourselves to others regularly, but are our conversations a mutual exchange to understanding? Do we articulate our feelings well while listening carefully to other people's ideas, thereby being an excellent communicator and problem solver?

With that said, how well do you know your spouse? In most relationships, couples like to think they have each other figured out, but there still could be a lot to learn even after years of being together. You will be pleasantly surprised to find out what your partner does or doesn't know about you. You may be married for years, and something could just come up that was never discussed.

So, how well do you know your best friend "BFF"? Admittedly, you'll say I know about everything! But maybe there are a few surprises in there. Well, considering its discovery time, here's an idea you should try with your favorite person. You only have to do it once; it's a list of questions to ask a friend that I think will bring your even closer.

You may see a whole new side of your BFF and may also give you some ideas on what to get him or her for their birthday or Christmas. Some questions I found on google and others are my questions. So, get to know your BFF, even more by asking him or her the following questions:

1. What is one thing you regret having done or not done in your life?

2. Where is the most beautiful place on earth and why?

3. Which parent do you identify with the most?

4. Is there anything I can do that will make your heart rest easier?

5. If you could change your first name what would it be?

6. What embarrasses you the most in front of other people?

7. If you had to choose one thing you were most passionate about, what would it be and why?

8. What was the name of the first person you ever had a crush on? Why did you like them?

9. What is your shoe size?

10. If you could buy one material thing, and money was not an issue, what would it be?

11. What's your favorite color?

12. What food will you absolutely not, under any circumstances eat?

13. What's the best way to comfort you when you're having a really terrible day?

14. Has anything/anyone every saved your life before?

15. Would you ever adopt a child?

16. What is one thing you're embarrassed to admit you want to try?

17. If you were a cake which cake would you be?

18. What is the most important material possession you have and why?

19. What is the most important memory you have and why?

20. When was the last time you cried?

21. How old was your mother when she had you?

22. Which famous person would you like to be BFFs with?

23. Is there something you wish you had said sorry for but never did?

24. What can you cook or bake the best?

Try this with your spouse or a parent and ask meaningful questions to stir up deep conversations. Write down questions; there are many different categories should give you an idea of what they know about you, and at the very least, get you talking. The more conversation, the better, so if one question spins off-topic, let it happen, you may discover more than you intended. Try this with an associate, friend, or anyone to get to understand them if they are willing to talk with you. Ask questions to see if they are open to speaking, not necessarily personal, but icebreaker things like, what project are you working on now, where is your next travel destination? Have you ever considered working for yourself?

Never underestimate the value of pleasant small talk as it might encourage someone, create a friendship, help, and even save a life physically and spiritually. We cannot achieve anything that is of significant value unless we cultivate a sincere heart to make a difference.

Do people like you when they meet you, and are they drawn to you? Can they see or feel your confidence, and do they listen? Are you likable, but not listened to? Are you insecure in one way or another? Does this cause you to overcompensate, withdraw, or completely fail to demonstrate value and impact on the world? Do you exude too much confidence, intelligence, and success without being human that it intimidates others and results in dislike and discourage others from liking you?

I challenge you to observe your own and others' behavior and consider the effect it has. Think about that for a moment. Below are things to remember when communicating and connecting with people:

- Smile and make eye contact.

- Use the person's name (make sure you know it).

- Give your name.

- Consider personal space (physical distance between two people).

- Ask questions (Go beyond impression).

- Keep things positive.

- Listen and show that you're listening (always wait for a response from the person).

•Look for signs of personality/behavior disorder (poor self-image, isolation, strange look in eyes or facial expression, anger, self-harm, negativity, depression). It's important to recognize signs to evaluate or to seek help or possibly alert the family.

•Be compassionate as Jesus was always moved with compassion.

Analytical Skills

• When dealing with others, these skills incorporate many skills like attention to detail, critical thinking ability, decision making, and researching in order to analyze a person and reason who they are. We all may not be proficient analytical, but this concept has everything to do with the ability to collect and analyze information, problem-solving, and make decisions.

• We can all do this!

• First, we must collect information through verbal communication. Talk and have more than small talk. Engage in conversations with someone, also, ask about spiritual life, preferable a relationship with God, not religion. You may need them to explain what's their meaning of spiritual or their relationship with God. It involves a systematic step-by-step approach to thinking that allows you to break down from different perspectives.

• Use a visual approach to be observant — Visually analyze their demeanor, attire, bruises, and other outer appearances such as hair, and skin.

• Observe people by using as many of your senses to see what's happening around them, their response and such.

• Learn how things work — It's more than finding the solution, but knowing how exactly certain things work.

• Practice your problem-solving skills — Keep in mind that there is a solution for every problem an individual has.

• Now that you have gathered all the information, you will see that demeanor, attire and other outer appearances may be a cover-up for what is going on internally.

• Analyze with the interpretation to know for sure by taking the time to understand what your results say. For example, — You use your critical thinking skills to assess whether someone is the real deal. Take the time to be patient and use your analytical skills to understand others.

Knowing who a person is does not matter if you don't have to develop a close relationship. When you have to spend time working together and problem-solving, knowing who is on your team is vital. When someone goes through their day-to-day in-character, it will work for a while, but eventually, they will reveal themselves. At the core of our being, our innermost circle, we are our true selves. This version is what you show to people you trust the most. With our nearest and dearest, we can give our honest opinions and express our real beliefs.

Being our authentic selves requires us to be vulnerable, so we are protected about our true nature. If you want to identify someone's character, examine how he or she treats others who can do nothing for them. Look at who they associate themselves with, and in a pressure situation, the choices one makes will reveal his or her real character.

Being Vulnerable

Most people are afraid to be vulnerable by letting someone see who they are and risk being rejected or feeling abandoned. Uncertainty is a given in every day of our lives and tied to anxiety or fear. It is only through allowing ourselves to be vulnerable that we can understand, feel empathy, forgive each other, and know that we are worthy of love and belonging.

Emotional courage is sharing our feelings with those who are important to us and accepting their feelings as valid and vital. Being vulnerable allows us to create new ideas and to see fresh possibilities previously blocked from our minds. We risk that our creations will be judged poorly or rejected and that we may feel shame or inadequate.

However, we risk failure to have the chance of success; and if you are vulnerable, you will see the best in people. You love others over the little things like how they smile because you give yourself the freedom to feel. Vulnerability means you are ,comfortable opening up to other people. You want others to know the authentic you instead of forcing a fake smile.

Vulnerability means you care deeply about things. You don't want to lose what you have because you love what you have. You love your life or at least certain parts of it, and you aren't willing to lose any pieces. You are eager to give someone your heart to provide them with the power to destroy or rebuild you.

Vulnerability means you're comfortable crying over the things that upset you instead of pushing away your emotions. You admit when you're upset instead of trying to put on an act and appear strong when you're secretly crumbling.

Vulnerability means you have nothing to hide; you have a clear understanding of who you are. You realize you are not indestructible or superhuman. You are mortal and full of flaws, but you're still beautiful.

Vulnerability means having a love for people you have never met. That we are all connected because we share common thoughts and beliefs.

Vulnerability means you have doubts. You think so highly of other people, of your friends and coworkers and parents, but it does mean that you see places where you can make improvements and try your hardest to do so. It does mean that sometimes we need to be able to connect with feelings that are evil in ourselves. It means we need to be willing to hurt just as much as someone else and be prepared to do this without anything to gain.

Have you been hurt in a relationship and you can't relate to any of these? You don't have to feel alone because God is with you in this and any situation.

Be Vulnerable with God

In the place of your real vulnerability with God, your perspective and your entire life is transformed. Let's see what happened to Peter as he was walking on water in his vulnerable moment.

"But straightway Jesus spoke unto them, saying, be of good cheer; it is I; be not afraid. And Peter answered him and said, Lord, if it be thou, bid me come unto thee on the water. And he said, come. And when Peter was come down out of the ship, he walked on the water, to go to Jesus. But when he saw the wind boisterous, he was afraid; and beginning to sink, he cried, saying, Lord, save me. And immediately Jesus stretched forth his hand, and caught him, and said unto him, O thou of little faith, wherefore didst thou doubt?" **—Matthew 14:27-31—KJV.**

Jesus did not compel Peter to come out but instead complied with his request to prove who Jesus said He is. Of course, Jesus is who He said, so, Peter does the impossible. Peter is fine until he starts looking at the waves and remembers his humanity. He forgot that walking on water is possible, as he's doing it, but he's in the middle of the water. Throw all of your faith in God and watch what will happen— running out of faith; trust God to save you.

Have you stepped out of the boat and feel like you can't do it all, and you need a miracle? God doesn't call us to a life that is safe and comfortable. You may ask the Lord, but if I step out of the boat, "**How many times will I look at the waves?** God's possible response, **plenty, but I have a plan for that!**" Peter forgot that before he focused on the waves, he was living his best life. It is when we focus on our humanity rather than Him that we start to sink. Peter said he couldn't do this, but he knew that before he got out of the boat. Peter was already doing the miracle he just needed to continue trusting Jesus.

Jesus saw something in Peter that He did not know in Himself. There is nothing like having someone believe in you when you are struggling to believe in yourself. Isn't it great to have someone who has caught a glimpse of your destiny as you still work with your history? There is nothing like having Jesus come along and give you the confidence to say yes to God. Peter became the first leader of the early church (a body of believers in a public assembly).

- God's love touched me so profoundly. I honestly could not have imagined Him to be the most stabilizing revelation of my life. The source would return to countless times over in moments of uncertainty and trouble.

- Remember, to be in a relationship with someone means we must communicate life, the good and the bad.

- Do you feel a draw to seek Him, then it's time to be vulnerable with God?

- Tell Him your desire to come to Him and then be honest with Him and yourself. Listen and obey whatever you need to do, and He will meet you at your need.

Your mind is the most powerful tool you have for creating good in your life, for without it, you cannot utilize your brain's thought process well for decisively thinking. However, if not used correctly, it can also be the most destructive force in your life.

You don't know someone without communicating, asking questions, being vulnerable, and using your brain to develop the raw facts and developing facts that are free from error or bias, which accurately represents knowledge of someone.

To Thy Own Self be True

The following quote, *"to thy own self be true"* is from *William Shakespeare's Hamlet*, in which Polonius is giving fatherly advice to his 18-year-old son. I think rather than accepting this phrase at face value, Shakespeare wanted us to look at it critically. It is still kind words to live by and sound advice that he did not follow.

Some people go through life, pretending to mask who they are. Thoughts that run through our heads can help us reach our dreams or draw us to our greatest fears. However, most people don't recognize the inherent power of their thoughts. We go about our lives absorbed in one mindset, without the clear realization that we move towards whatever we think about or focus on consistently, we move towards.

Polonius believes that a person can be harmless and useful to others when he is financially sound. Therefore, he must be loyal to his best interest first, then take care of others.

The first meaning is that someone can better judge themselves if they have done what they should or could have done. The second meaning is that one must be honest in his ways and relations. The third meaning is that one must always do the right thing. Doing the right thing is used in honesty and commitment when someone tries to cheat them.

A Different Perspective

Bosses use it in their offices, lecturing their employees not to waste time, while parents use it to warn their children to refrain from keeping bad company. Service and production companies also use this, showing their commitment, dedication, and adherence to quality and standard. I believe this phrase has become the motto of modern America, where self has become the primary standard for truth.

Regardless of what people think Shakespeare meant, his meaning is to be true and honest to yourself. Society will tell you to be yourself that life isn't about finding yourself; it's about creating yourself. That you are unique, amazing, and there isn't another person like you. While there is truth in being unique, life is more than about creating yourself.

We cannot ignore that our mantra has become to take care of number one. We are involved in a continual love affair with ourselves. However, the discussion we need to have is how we come to know and love ourselves. If you love yourself and love your neighbor as yourself, it will reflect well in your relationships. Life is a continuous process of knowing who we are or discovering our true selves.

Self-discovery is satisfying, but can also be a painful experience in understanding one self and navigating correctly throughout life. This is where most people stop their growth by not first discovering their true self. Nevertheless, once you know what you have found, you must measure it by God's standard.

"For all have sinned and fall short of the glory of God."—
Romans 3:23 —this is the reason you need the help that only Jesus can give you. He alone can make you what you ought to be.

The process of self-discovery requires an undoing of the self-knowledge that you assume you already knew. Life is not something that happens to us but through, with, and for us. The hard part for most people is to take responsibility and embrace this new way of seeing life from the inside out. It is not a new concept because you were born with everything you need to succeed.

We are so conditioned to look outside of ourselves for fulfillment and answers that we become totally disconnected from our own individuality. I think this is why depression and anxiety have a lot to do with our sudden increase with teen and adult low self-esteem.

While our outward appearance is well dressed, we neglect our inner self. Self-discovery should be an important goal for everyone. Don't become what others want you to be. Know thyself is only through the discovery to identify our purpose and actualize our potential. It's time to take a self-discovery of yourself, but not to worry, no one will be privy to or evaluate it but you.

You may even embark on revealing something unrecognizable about yourself or discover something about us all. Each of us is uniquely different individually, but the same in our understanding of continuous self-awareness.

Who are you? It sounds like an easy question to answer, right? No one can define you; you're the only one who gets to say who you are. Knowing yourself is essential, some things are apparent and some are not. Taking a look at you can help you learn what your hidden treasures are and share it with the world if you haven't.

On the flip side, you will discover a darker side about yourself, and that's ok (we all have a dark side), but I want you to understand its origin.

Focus on your Strengths but Know your Weakness.

To be true to ourselves, we must know our strengths and our weakness to ensure our financial, spiritual, and social success. We cannot focus on our strengths and neglect our weakness because both are a part of our makeup. Your strengths must out way your weakness, but both are there as a balance within us all.

What are your Strengths?

Your strengths are a mixture of your talents, knowledge, skills, and something you enjoy doing. Everyone has strengths, put them to work, so you will find new ways to unleash your potential. If you focus on your strengths, you will do better in life because satisfaction is doing what you enjoy. Remember, as you flow in your purpose, people are looking to use you to advance themselves. Some people are self-driven with their vision to make a name for themselves at your detriment.

What are your Weaknesses?

You know what you avoid and what you could be doing better. For instance, you manage eight people, but you don't like to delegate tasks, and you don't like confrontation. It bothers me when you are busy doing most of the work yourself to avoid delegating or resolving interpersonal issues.

You may not think that the inability to say no, being disorganized, smoking, excessive drinking are weaknesses. Know your weaknesses so that you can overcome it, but don't let your body govern you. If you don't know your weaknesses, step number one is to gain self-awareness, whether through a coach, personality assessment, or feedback from your family or friends. Ask them what you don't do well or any bad habits you may have.

Target a specific behavior that you need to change then work hard at breaking that behavior. If you have to post stickers on your bathroom window, listen to motivating teachings, do not go back to the old way of doing things. The problem with us is that we are lazy, we want to look sharp and shine in our strengths, while our weakness drags us down in shame.

There is no easy way around to deal with your weaknesses, don't ignore, outsource it or play it down because failure is inevitable. You can do this!

- If you need help get an accountability partner but don't let your weaknesses bring down your strengths.

- I'm not here to judge, just to help you find out about you and destroy any issues hindering your progress in life.

- It will take you digging deep into your childhood to reveal the good/bad experiences that have shaped you. Please, give thought to this because most of our issues stems from our childhood up-bringing.

- What happened in your yesterday is important in your today.

- The results of your yesterdays may be causing you great pain and sadness.

- It is important to realize what your beliefs are if good and live by them.

- This is not an easy journey as you have to literally re-visit all your choices in life.

- Whereas, it's spring cleaning of the mind, your emotions and your surroundings to include people in your life.

- It requires making some tough decisions and sticking to them.

You may have to cut people out of your life who do not bring value to your life, such as takers. Think about what baggage of personal hurt you won't let go of to start the healing process. Are you following your passion or whatever you enjoy doing and begin to look within yourself for answers? Only when we define ourselves by God's Word rather than the thinking and experiences of the world can we discover our deepest identity.

As Albert Einstein who said *"We cannot solve our problems with the same level of thinking that created them."*

Now that you are convinced that self-knowledge is worth having (not that you needed to be convinced). Here are the summary benefits:

- Teach others how to treat you — The way you treat yourself sets the standards of what you expect from others. Treat yourself with respect, talk nicely too, and about yourself. You protect who you are and who you want to become.

- Happiness — You are happier when you can express who you are. Expressing your desires will likely get you what you want.

- Less inner conflict — When your outside actions are in peace with your inside feelings and values, you will experience less internal conflict.

- Better decision-making — When you know yourself, you can make better choices about everything, from small decisions to big decisions like which partner you'll spend your life with. You'll have guidelines to apply to solve life's diverse problems.

- Self-control — When you know yourself, you understand what motivates you to resist bad habits and develop good ones.

- Resistance to social pressure self-control — When you know yourself, you understand what motivates you to resist bad habits and develop good ones.

- When you are grounded in your value of self, you are more likely to say no to peer or societal pressure.

- Tolerance and understanding of others — Being aware of your struggles can help you empathize with others.

- Have compassion for yourself and others — Accept people as they are and listen intending to find out new things, understanding, and seeing the person in front of you. Sometimes, the person in front of you is you. See yourself, acknowledge when life is tough for you, and hug yourself. Again, give a hug to your soul free from judgment, blame or guilt. Keep in mind you and those around you are only human.

- When you take yourself too seriously, you believe everything revolves around you. But everyone makes mistakes even though this seems to be something dumb; you will have another chance to get things right, so learn the lesson from what you have been through.

- Almost everything that happens in life has a positive side. Search for that side of things and be confident that whatever life puts in front of you, you'll find your way.

It's hard to remain true to yourself because you are continually changing, and society's values often conflict with our own. On the other hand, failure to embark on a life journey of self—discovery will rob us of the opportunity to understand who we are and how we can help others on their pilgrimage in life. With that said, let's be honest with ourselves so people can begin to know you instead of seeing your pretend mask. If we outgrow pretending, a new kind of self can exist whose foundation is freedom with an authentic creation of self. Knowing yourself is quite possible the meaning of life in finding out who you are in Christ.

In our self-discovery journey, Father God, I pray we see ourselves as sons and daughters worthy of your love. We forgive ourselves for any self-inflicted mistakes that may have caused us to lose, suffer, anger, or frustration because we purpose to live our lives without seeking your wisdom. We forgive and make peace with ourselves, and we forgive anyone who has hurt us. Father help us see ourselves in the light of your love as **Jeremiah 29:11 NIV** says,

"For I know the plans I have for you declares the Lord, plans to prosper you and not to harm you, plans to give you hope and a future."

In Jesus Name. Amen!

Perspective

S omeone walking up the stairs might complain about walking instead of using the elevator while the other person might get excited about the chance to build strength and keep fit. How do two different people have such vastly, differing opinions? Why does one person believe everything is beautiful, and another one thinks life is chaotic and out of control?

The environment can be the same, but the one thing that will seldom be the same is our perception. Your perspective defines your experience. It's good to keep this in mind because just this one statement can redefine your entire mood. Everyone has an angle or a point of view based on your personality and experiences. We don't share the same basic experiences in our lives.

The reality is that we live in our personalities; our lives are a constant stream of our thoughts going through our minds. The fact that we all observe and experience our lives via the thoughts in our head demonstrates our sameness. With that said, your perspective may not be entirely accurate as it relates to another. Our differences should be personality traits, interests, foods, culture, but not values and ethics.

Everyone either has an objective or subjective view, whenever you interact with someone. If you have a subjective perspective, it's often influenced by personal feelings, verses being based on facts. An objective viewpoint, however, is based in truth and not influenced by your personal bias. The saying *"beauty is in the eye of the beholder"* is an example of a subjective view. Your subjective personal or professional view if spoken from a place of hurt will leave others feeling wounded. The problem with a subjective view is that unknown truth is not always revealed to us about someone. This is vital to the understanding of what a person is really like thereby knowing what to expect and how to assist him/her. Don't be that person who renders your personal opinion without facts.

Imagine you idealize a person to the point where you see him or her as more than human, as superior to you and larger than life. You admire him or her from afar and never really try to connect with him or her or genuinely get to know or understand them. Idealizing other people appeases them and makes you feel inferior. There are many people who idealize pastors, celebrities, or other people they look up to and love. It's acceptable behavior for a child to idealize their parents, but not so much for an adult to idealize another flawed human being.

Of all the species, humans are the most flawed, but we are certainly the most beautiful. Some flaws are simply part of you, they make you unique, and they make you attractive. Flaws like the gap between your front teeth, your prominent forehead, and your pointy nose are not worth the stress because you dislike them. When you acknowledge that these flaws are not going to change, you will find the value in them. Beauty is an expression of perfection, but it is imperfection that leads to beauty.

Don't give someone the power to make you feel weak because they might not like one of your qualities. There are flaws like being an addict or an abusive person, which will be transformed when surrendered to God. As humans we are imperfect people. The good news is that in the Bible, God chose flawed or imperfect people to spread His truth.

People are not what you think when their flaws impair them. God loves you, and He created you and desires you enough to see past your imperfections.

We Do not Create Truth; we Receive it from Our Creator

God is the giver, and every gift He offers is based on His knowledge of us, our attitude is to be that of receiving from Him all the time, and in this way, we become sons and daughters of God. It requires effort and produces the greatest humility to receive anything from God because we would much rather earn it. God does not expect us to earn our salvation because redemption has already been paid through Christ. Receive what God has done instead of making a case for why God should give to me.

Let's take a Look at What is Going on Inside of Us

Brokenness is an unspoken word in most conversations, and many people remain unnoticed in this state for years. We substitute alcohol, drugs, sex, material things, and even work in an attempt to numb our feelings. Brokenness is a result of our struggle with our sinful nature. We all struggle with our sinful human nature in some way every day. All of humanity has fallen out of friendship with God leaving us diseased and dying in every part of our personalities and bodies. Through our reflection of His likeness into shattered, distorted images, our suffering is the result of our brokenness. None of this was God's original plan for humanity. Through Jesus Christ, God is repairing His Creation.

He called the broken, the faithless, and the poor in spirit to do great things in His name. Don't believe me; read the bible? There are many stories of people who are too numerous to discuss imperfect people whose lives were changed through faith in Christ. Philemon, a book in the Bible (New Testament) spoke of Onesimus who lived as a slave, Onesimus had wronged Philemon and was now in prison. While there, he met Paul and came to faith in Christ. He was a changed man, but Onesimus was still a runaway slave owned by Philemon.

Paul had explained the gospel to Philemon and had witnessed the profound result of a once-dead heart to a new life. Paul reminded Philemon that he was to accept the newly converted Onesimus back, not as a lawbreaker or his slave, but as a fellow brother in Christ. His letter to Philemon presents the beautiful and majestic transition from slavery to the kinship that comes from Christian love and forgiveness. — **Philemon 1:8-19 —Paraphrased.**

Many years ago, I met a man who had recently been released from prison, who was fighting alcohol and drug addictions. He was living in a home that helped former prisoners return to society. Though he was now clean and sober, some people still rejected him because they couldn't get past the old nature of this newly transformed person. We may be able to improve our lives somewhat, but to lift ourselves out of brokenness and become whole without turning to God, is close to impossible; and we will fail.

Another reason People Are Not What You Think is that society has women obsessed with their physical appearance. Women are generally more concerned about their looks or appearance than men because they are judged more on their looks than men and taught that their looks matter more from a very young age. This mindset is embedded in women, so it's not surprising that massive insecurity is the outcome. The truth is that women's insecurities about their appearance often result in competition with other women.

This obsession with beating their competition at any cost has caused some women to damage their health with their desire to be skinner, thinking this will attract men, while their health is compromised. The perception that we must be sexier is why attractive women are featured more in advertisements. Women also spend vast amounts of money on clothes, cosmetics, and other products and services that enhance their physical appearance. Being whole is from the inside, so you're a true reflection of yourself on the outside.

People are not what you think when their imperfections are either visible or unseen. An undesirable feature in a person's character began within before it becomes a physical attribute. Let that sink in for a moment. I love this Japanese perspective on beauty—Wabi-sabi is simple *"a view of the world, where the beauty of things is imperfect, impermanent and incomplete." "Beauty within us and around us, which might be hidden or overlooked, subtle and silent, as we go on with our hectic lifestyles."* —Wikipedia.

Nathan H. Lents, PHD said *"Rather than doom and gloom, a full accounting of our glitches and limitations provides clues on how to live in better harmony with a body that was shaped for a very different world. A world where we are not created to be flawed but perfect with God in every way."* Wow, this is good!

Despite our many flaws, we have accomplished so much that the fight is worth it. Expecting our bodies or minds to be perfect is not reasonable while on earth. A pastor once said, *"The church is perfect until you get there."* There is no ideal church (body of believers).

Churches are made up of and led by humans—fallen and broken people. We all want to someday attend that perfect ideal church. Throughout the Bible, God uses imperfect people and as it still stands today, there's only One perfect man.

God has something much greater for imperfect people, places, and positions; He wants to sanctify us to the perfect image of His Son. If we are conformed to Christ's Image, Christ become more and more the Center of all things in our lives. Paul said that when he was weak, through Christ, he was made strong. Strong through his infirmities and his imperfections.

There have been men and women much used of God who have fallen into satanic traps or their own snares because of moral weaknesses. You would think, how can they be anointed and mightily used of God? God's precious anointing did not prevent them from being exposed to the world and the influence of temptation since temptation is common to all men. **—1 Corinthians 10:13 —Paraphrased.**

Failure did not occur because the Spirit of God was not there, but because the person submitted (surrendered) to the tempter. It is the spirit that is alive through repentance; the flesh must still be put under subjection. I often marvel at God's incredible grace to extend His love for humanity even as we overcome obstacle-after-obstacle.

In the book Paper Towns by John Green, he said, "When did we see each other face-to-face? Not until you saw into my cracks, and I saw into yours. Before that, we were just looking at ideas of each other."

While accepting others' mistakes is part of letting go of the past and viewing others with compassion, this is more about you making allowance for your own mistakes, not feeling haunted by regrets, and afraid to move forward in your life. Yes, you may have made some mistakes in the past that you need to resolve with yourself and others, but if your overall attitude towards yourself is one of constant criticism, seeing only your mistakes rather than what you achieved, you are essentially living in an abusive relationship with yourself. Your quality of life is, therefore, subjective and varies based on what makes you satisfied.

No standard defines happiness for everyone; each person has their own definition of happiness. What do you want from your life; what are your expectations and goals? Remember, your thoughts are powerful.

How would your world change if you believe you are capable of anything? What would you change about yourself if you trusted that the opportunity to live your dream would present itself? The world is precisely what you think it is because your thoughts frame your reality. The second you realize that, you take power over your life. This is not the totality of everything that is required, however, there must be corresponding action and behavior.

Everything you have ever learned and experienced every second you have been alive has contributed to the way you experience your life today. The key is in accepting ourselves in all aspects and not insisting on deceiving our conscience.

Another perspective is people are good if your perception is that of good. As a child, I have heard it said, that we are to see the good in everyone. Absolutely, there is good in everyone, but don't blind side yourselves with the notion that everyone is good. Jesus answered the rich young ruler about being good. Let's look at **Mark 10:17-22—KJV.**

"And when he was gone forth into the way, there came one running, and kneeled to him, and asked him, 'Good Master, what shall I do that I may inherit eternal life? And Jesus said unto him, Why callest thou me good? there is none good but one, that is, God. Thou knowest the commandments, Do not commit

A Different Perspective

adultery, Do not kill, Do not steal, Do not bear false witness, Defraud not, Honour thy father and mother. And he answered and said unto him, Master, all these have I observed from my youth. Then Jesus beholding him loved him, and said unto him, One thing thou lackest: go thy way, sell whatsoever thou hast, and give to the poor, and thou shalt have treasure in heaven: and come, take up the cross, and follow me. And he was sad at that saying, and went away grieved: for he had great possessions."'

This encounter between Jesus and this man recorded in the books of Matthew, Mark, and Luke is pivotal because it deals with such a critical issue for us to understand. Superficial interest in eternal life must be confronted. The central point of this encounter is pride and selfishness, no matter how much he said he wanted eternal life, he was not prepared to do what was required to receive it. This young man failed the most critical test of his life. He was offered a choice between himself and God, between fulfillment here and now and fulfillment in the life to come. The question was, what was more valuable to him? God and the life to come? Or his own will and the present life?

The bottom line is, the rich young ruler wanted eternal life, but not enough to give up his pride and possessions. He never questioned the truthfulness of what Jesus said; he didn't speak his mind; he didn't argue; he just walked away. It is very evident that which Jesus was offering was going to cost him his pride, and his possessions, and to him, the price was too high, even in exchange for eternal life. He wanted eternal life only to complement what he already possessed; He loved himself, not God. He loved earth; not heaven. He loved the material; not the spiritual. The issue here is salvation. Eternal life equals salvation, and he wanted to take possession of salvation based solely on his terms.

This man was already at the point where he knew there was eternal life, and he knew he wanted it instead of its alternative, eternal death. This was a spiritual pursuit for him, but he was unprepared for Jesus's answer.

"That's the gospel Christ took your punishment, paid for your sins, and gave you His perfect goodness."

It is receiving what was already done through Christ, so it's not of your works that anyone can boast. Jesus used a penetrating question to push him to think past his own words, to understand the concept of Jesus' goodness and, his own lack of goodness. Did the young man miss it? He realized that although he had devoted himself to keeping the commandments, he had failed to keep the first and greatest of the commandments. *"Jesus said unto him, Thou shalt love the Lord thy God with all thy heart, and with all thy soul, and with all thy mind."* —**Matthew 22:37**—KJV. This had nothing to do with keeping his riches because it is God who gives us the power to be wealthy. God desires for you to prosper financially. God did not have this young man's whole heart nor was he ready to commit himself to something greater than him.

When you are in love with someone, you agree to give yourself to the relationship and everything that it involves. He quite simply was not ready to experience this kind of relationship, yet felt it necessary to inquire of Jesus. The rich young ruler could have kept his possessions and freely received salvation if he were willing to pursue Christ.

The problem is that we miss the whole point of our existence, the very purpose for which God Created us. God made us for the relationship of His perfect love. But if we're always chasing after other things, we will never experience the fullness of that love. There's a big difference between a half-hearted approach to God and whole-hearted devotion. Do we want to walk in the fullness of His love and His plans; or, do we want to spend our lives following (chasing) after the world's empty pleasures?

Are we letting this world and all of its demands and distractions crowd God out? Do our lives give evidence of godliness? Without really understanding that God is with us, He is sovereign, He is all seeing, He is all knowing, we think that we can get away with even murder!

If we really think about God, and care about what He thinks, then it is not just a matter of intellectual thought, but also a matter of understanding what God wants us to do and be willing to do it. Like the rich young ruler, it wasn't that he believed God didn't exist, but that he lived his life as if God didn't exist. In man's thoughts there is no room for God. — **Paraphrased—Psalms 10:4—KJV.**

"Are you a rich young ruler? Do you live your life as if God doesn't exist? Do you have a form of godliness, but your life denies the power thereof?" As believers, I think we may need to examine how we portray God so that we do not find ourselves walking away defeated like the rich young ruler! **Selah.**

What Do You Think?

A tall, handsome young man is standing at the entrance of a shopping center in any city, providence, state, or county in the USA. He is about twenty-something-years-old, no facial expression, with a white top hat on his head. I prefer not to give his race or nationality because I want you to focus without bias. Boldly printed in red on the center of his top hat are the words "**I AM ANGRY**."

I wondered if people would notice the hat on his head or be concerned about reading what's written on it. I asked seven men and seven women at random if they saw this man outside of a mall wearing a top hat, what would be their perception.

Four men and one woman said they thought it was marketing to promote a hat. One of the seven women I asked focused on the attractiveness of the young man. Her focus was on his looks and not on his top hat. Two men said, they just did not care because their focus was on shopping rather than reading what's written on a hat. One woman thought it may be a cry for help and would approach him to try to understand what was wrong. One man and four women said they would run away because of the statement on his hat.

What would you do if you saw that? Would you say murderers and angry people don't broadcast their anger? They do, but we don't always hear their words, or maybe we were just too busy to notice, or care, or help. It's more than what is written on the hat, although vital because it tells you the man's state. Is he broadcasting the truth about himself, but people either misinterpret or don't see it? Is he an angry man, is this proof that people are not what you think? Your mind, or more precisely your thoughts, affects your perception and, therefore, your interpretation of reality.

Invisible Influence

N aturally, looking into a mirror and realizing your spiritual identity isn't a normal occurrence. The physical world reminds us daily that we are humans with five senses, telling us what we hear, see, feel, smell and taste. We see ourselves as humans instead of spiritual beings first.

The *Barna Group* is an evangelical Christian polling firm; their research shows that most people don't believe in the devil nor the Holy Spirit. *"The study examined how one segment of the Christian population—those whose beliefs about salvation categorize them as "born again"—differ from the beliefs of people who describe themselves as Christian, but do not base their view of salvation solely on confession of sin and God's grace received through Jesus Christ."* Barna said, *"Americans are constantly trying to figure out how to make sense of biblical teachings in light of their daily experiences."*

Without realizing it, we have become highly critical human beings concerned with body image and other trivial issues and not our spirit. Jesus assured His disciples that the Holy Spirit would stay by their side; the unseen hand of God, known as the Helper, the Healer to aid His people. As human beings, we operate as three-part beings, body, soul, and spirit. God and an evil presence (devil) are spiritual beings, and we are also spiritual beings (because we have a spirit) that lives in our human bodies (flesh) possess a soul (mind, emotions, and feelings). Think about this: both God (good) and the enemy (evil) strive to influence your thoughts.

Now, what makes it tricky for most people is because feelings are the result of specific life events. For example, if a loved one passes away, you feel loss, grief and maybe even hopelessness. Though we may be in denial, decisions based on life events are a direct correlation to our feelings which can be spirit led by an invisible influence.

We come into this world with an innate wisdom of our spiritual nature, but through life as it unfolds, we forget who and how magnificent we are. Every breath which God breathed into man which became a living soul has God's DNA. We have separated ourselves from God because of our human nature, but God never separated Himself from us. It is the nature of sin that brings about shame like Adam and Eve who hid from God after their disobedience. First of all, separation from God is an impossibility with Him being omnipresent. Honoring God is bringing ourselves closer to the love of God because His grace is wider and deeper still. —**Romans 5:20— paraphrased.**

It was God who called Adam and Eve to acknowledge their wrongdoings, repent (turn away from) and allow God's Spirit to cleanse and make them whole. He is the one who desires to join Himself to us. God is a Spirit who communicates with us through our spirit, and then our spirit communicates what we hear.

It is similar to a thought or a prompting, which to a believer is called an inward witness. Most of the time, when we refer to ourselves in the flesh, we refer to our bodies. Once born again, our *spirit man becomes brand new,* recreated in the very Image and Likeness of God. If you want to mature as a believer, you must learn to develop who you are in Him; the renewal of your mind, not *your flesh.* The first key to growing is to become Holy Spirit conscious; we must renew our minds through the Word of God. Praying in the spirit is the easiest way as a believer to instantly allow your spirit to become the dominant part of your three-part being. In other words, we rely on the spirit to pray.

Secondly, we are to imitate Him as His children. We do so by walking in love just as Jesus walked in love. Walking in God's love means we treat others the way we would want to be treated, no matter how they treat us. The very first fruit of our spirit is God's love. When we choose to yield to the love of God, we are yielding to our spirit.

Our fascination with our thoughts makes us forget our true nature as spiritual beings; but some thoughts are not helpful, and we can't pay attention to every thought that occurs. Thoughts just happen; it is up to us how we want to be in a relationship with the thoughts that compete for our attention. We don't want to abandon our emotions with just our thoughts and disconnect from our senses. The mind turns now into a bundle of thoughts, a concept, something to talk about, and something we dissolve into.

Allowing another voice (enemy) to enter through the portal of your spirit will eventually decide what reaches your mind. It's very subtle, and if you cater to accepting evil or the voice of the enemy, you will become whatever he initiates. The enemy's voice brings confusion, fear, compromise, and guilt. On the other hand, God's Voice is very gentle and to hear Him; He requires a closeness with Him and regular practice to hear clearly and more quickly. That's why the more time you spend with God and practice tuning into His Voice, the more it will become easy to recognize and obey. God's Voice is calm, encouraging, loving, and peaceful.

God is omnipotent—He is all-powerful.

God is omniscient—He is all-knowing.

God is omnipresent—He is present everywhere.

The devil, in contrast, does not reflect these divine attributes. While God can be everywhere at the same time, satan cannot; he can only be in one place at a time. Though satan has powers, he's not more powerful than any man, nor is he more powerful than the angels assigned to us; he is nothing more than an imitator. The enemy would want you to believe he's as powerful as God but he's not anywhere near to being equal with God because he is all evil in contrast to God being all Love.

There is a spiritual battle for your mind between good and evil, but the choice to obey is through your will. Our choice is called free will which exists in all humanity, and was given to us by God. God chooses not to control our free will, and the devil has never been able to. There are two voices always speaking to your mind to influence your thoughts. Your desire or choice is to either obey the Voice of God or the devil.

Only one can become the dominant voice of reasoning to your thoughts, what you see, and your actions. You have to tune out one and receive the other. When a person kills, we ask, "What mental disorder does this person have?" Something has affected their thinking, mood, and feelings and has resulted in this unthinkable behavior. There is an evil spirit that causes a severe interruption in thought and behavior, resulting in an inability to cope with ordinary life. Some of the common disorders are depression, bipolar disorder, dementia, schizophrenia, and anxiety disorders. The individual may seem healthy at first, but they are not what you think! The disease is in the mind, but it's communicated through that person's spirit. Doctors use this term as a *defense mechanism.*

A defense mechanism "is an unconscious psychological mechanism that reduces anxiety arising from unacceptable or potentially harmful stimuli. Defense mechanisms may result in healthy or unhealthy consequences depending on the circumstances and frequency with which the mechanism is used."[1]

In other words, our defense mechanism kicks in to make us feel better about ourselves and making it easier for others to accept us; helping us to survive. Don't ignore your emotions, but remember that feelings aren't facts. Sometimes you have to rise above your feelings. For example, I awoke tired when I had a presentation at work, *"Do I ignore my feelings and arise*

---

[1] www.wikipedia

to give my awesome presentation or allow my feelings to override?"

Our ego defenses are natural because God put them there to help us keep disturbing or threatening thoughts from becoming conscious. If they get out of proportion, anxiety, phobias, obsessions, or hysteria may develop. I believe our defense mechanism is there to reason, and allow you to choose which way you wish to proceed with your thoughts. It's our choice to allow positive feelings to arise in place of fear and uncertainty. If you go to great lengths to consciously or unconsciously defend yourself, it will produce a negative craving.

It will become evident to everyone except you that you desperately try to make yourselves look good by explaining why your arguments or actions are justified. Because we become someone we are not, but appear and speak as if we are okay, this can be dangerous. God is a spirit who speaks to us through our spirit; check your receiver. You have to be expecting and ready to hear from Him to receive. Find His frequency, most of the time we are looking to hear some big revelation. God gives simple instructions about the small things in your life that you need to change. He will deal with you where you are, which involves helping you walk in His best by getting rid of things that are holding you back.

In order to learn to discern His Voice, you need to spend time with Him. It isn't just talking to Him (prayer), we learn His Voice when we listen (and obey). Align what you hear with the word of God. *"For the word of God is living and powerful, and sharper than any two-edged sword, piercing even to the division of soul and spirit, and of joints and marrow, and is a discerner of the thoughts and intents of the heart."*—**Hebrews 4:12—KJV.**

God will never tell you to do, think, or say anything contrary to His Word. First, you have to know His Word and keep it continually in your ear. Hearing God's Voice should be a lifestyle occurrence and not an occasional event. God wants you to hear His Voice, be still, and listen for His Voice. If you expect Him to speak and you listen for it, He will talk to you regularly.

As we walk in the spirit, we will not fulfill the lust of our flesh. Our spirit man begins to dominate our entire being and we become more aware of who we really are. We live by faith and not according to our human reasoning. Rather, let God's Word pierce and divide between what you are absorbing through your senses. Especially through your feelings and the wisdom that is from above, which you absorb through your spirit.

Through my spirit I am in contact with God. However, when I am in my flesh, I live according to my understanding, my senses, which are earthly. The spirit is not limited, but the body is and, therefore, has to catch up with the spirit. It's easy to distinguish our body from our spirit or even from our soul because the body is visible.

With the body, we interact with the physical realm;

With our spirit, we interact with the spiritual realm.

What about distinguishing our spirit, from our soul? It's much more difficult to distinguish between our spirit and our soul because they are intangible, unseen parts of our being. Yet, it is vitally important that we learn how to correctly distinguish between the two. Through the soul (reason, consciousness, memory, perception, thinking, senses, feelings), I am a social being in contact with people, and through the spirit I can relate with God and He with me.

If we don't have this fellowship with God, we won't be able to successfully listen to our heart, and be led by the Holy Spirit in any given situation and circumstances of our lives. This is why we seem different to others from who we are created to be because our spirit is not connected with God and we are walking in our flesh. Salvation through Christ is meant to change our relationship so that our spirit is made alive with His, allowing us to have healthy thoughts/emotions and be in peace within our mind.

You Don't Know My Heart

We think with our mind, we experience deep emotions (fear, anger, love, hate) in our hearts. If you allow negative thoughts, they will create negative images that we act upon. Whether these thoughts are expressed or not, they can still cause hurt, anger or sadness.

We are probably more comfortable with some of our thoughts than we are with others. It's important to understand them and to know that we can change the negative thoughts if we choose to. Your unconscious mind is continuously feeding thoughts and ideas into your emotions, thereby controlling your conscious mind.

Matthew 12:34—*"... For out of the abundance of the heart the mouth speaks."* And, **Mark 7:21—KJV** —*"For from within, out of the heart of men, proceed evil thoughts, adulteries, fornications, murders."*

It is important for us to maintain a pure heart before God. The phrase, *"guard your heart"* is crucial in protecting your emotions. In Christian circles, this saying carry weight, but needs more practical application especially to those between ages 12 and 25. If you teach your children as early as preschool how to guard their heart they will be prepared for the emotions of adolescent. Teach your children to do more than just avoid situations that cause physical pain, but to also protect that which is even more important—their heart.

A Different Perspective

Guarding your heart is simply protecting the deepest parts of you, your emotions, affections and your spirit.

Proverbs 4:23—NIV— *"Above all else, guard your heart, for everything you do flows from it."* Your heart determines your life. This is one of the most important proverbs. Any blessing or grief in your life depends on ruling and training your heart. If you direct and instruct your heart with Godly guidance, there is no limit to your potential success before God and man. Every offense starts in your heart, and your character and speech reflect your heart. You can only pretend to be different than your heart for a short time, for it will quickly regain control and dictate your actions. Besides, others can judge your heart by your words and choices.

Our character is made up of all sorts of habits and practices. These sets of habits and practices are woven together like the fibers of a rope. But when part of a rope unravels because of our habits, the integrity of the whole rope is at risk. It doesn't matter that most of the rope is fine what matters is the part that is not.

God taught us this lesson through the story of King David's anointing. Israel wanted a king so God sent the prophet Samuel to David's house to anoint the next king. Samuel did not at first choose David. Samuel spotted one of David's brothers who was tall and handsome so he thought this must be the one. But God told him NO!

Let's take a look at why God said NO. **1 Samuel 16:7**—**NIV.** *"But the Lord said to Samuel, 'Do not consider his appearance or his height, for I have rejected him. The Lord does not look at* *the things people look at. People look at the outward appearance, but the Lord looks on the heart.'"*

David was a man after God's own heart—**Acts 13:22**—NKJV—**paraphrased**. His heart was pointed toward God he had a deep desire to follow God's will and do everything God wanted him to do. As David kept his heart, you can keep your heart as well. Remember, he was careful and faithful to examine himself, to confess his sins, to pray, to delight in God's words, to choose Godly friends, to give thanks and sing praises to God. These heart exercises will keep your heart just and righteous and bring God's favor.

Your heart is your greatest asset, for it can do more for you than anything else. It is much more than the muscle beating 70 times a minute in your chest. Learn to set your affections on good things (**Colossians 3:2; Matthew 6:21**). You can keep your heart good, or you can let it become bad. You can be diligent in this project, or you can be lazy. God's children have an old man that tempts them to evil, but their new man calls them to godliness; your heart must often decide between the two.

Every person makes a series of choices each day, but those things which proceed out of the mouth come forth from the heart and they defile the man. *"These are the things which defile a man: but to eat with unwashen hands defileth not a man."* **Matthew 15:18-19—KJV**.

Though I don't claim to have all the answers, God really challenged my heart on this subject during my dating years. Establishing emotional boundaries, a set of *do's* and *don'ts* that guides you through the exchange of emotions without going too deep too fast. In other words, take your time in any relationship not to give out too much too soon, observing behaviors, weighing out other opinions and really listening to your spirit over your feelings. Hurt-people-hurt people; you can't see into one's heart unless God reveals it. However, if you pay attention to what people are saying they will literally tell you what is in their heart. Most of the time you are not listening or don't want to believe what has been spoken. Don't allow hurt people to damage your emotions and wound your spirit.

There are people who are babes which are growing so we give special considerations because they are learning. However, everyone's growth process is their own and some people will never do what it takes to mature. Our task is to stay focus on Jesus for He is the author and finisher of our faith. Don't be distracted with someone else's growth or the lack of, have a plan and focus on your developing physical, spiritual and financial growth.

Jeremiah 17:9 — *"The heart is deceitful above all things, and desperately wicked; who can know it?"* Your moral conduct of your life, and actions, are determined by the condition of your heart. In other words, you won't know your heart without acknowledging how you have nurtured and what you have placed inside of it.

Psalm 139:23-24 — *"Search me, O God, and know my heart; Try me, and know my anxieties; And see if there is any wicked way in me, And lead me in the way everlasting."*

A Different Perspective

David's confession is that God knew him better than he knew himself, and that he needed God to search and know him. David trusted only God to examine him and reveal the darkest corners of his heart. This showed how much he cared for holiness in his life, and how humble he was in recognizing there could be an unknown sin in him. David is declaring truth in trusting the God of complete knowledge will lead to everlasting life.

How to guard your heart *"And be not conformed to this world: but be ye transformed by the renewing of your mind..."* — **Romans 12:2a—KJV**.

When God gets ready to change someone, He changes how they think. God changes the thought process. What Solomon said to his son was, *"son guard, protect, and be careful of your thought life. Keep your heart with all diligence; for out of it are the issues of life."* Solomon is warning his son about the sexual affairs of a young man, having impure, immoral thoughts in his heart. He is saying Jesus can cure the mind and the body of their craving for the things that destroy.

Begin the process of changing the way you think and you will change your life. The Lord Jesus Christ wants us to present our bodies and minds to Him, that He might transform us. No wonder the enemy battles for the mind.

It is important that we learn to keep our hearts because a fierce battle is raging for the control of your mind.

How do you keep from thinking what's wrong? By having right thoughts. And if you're thinking what's right, you cannot be thinking what's wrong. In other words, load up on God's Word.

When the heart is right with God, you will see the fruit. God wants to minister to you; He wants to govern your speech—**Hebrews 4:24;** guard your sight—**v25;** guide your steps—**v27.** Make it a habit to read your Bible and other good books, to gain knowledge which the mind can feed upon constantly. If you are constantly hearing and feeding upon positive things, you will bring forth positive results. Feed the mind. Do it on purpose.

God has a wonderful plan for you, as you read the book of Proverbs, He will show you His plan for having health, wealth, and wisdom. It all begins in your thought life. It is impossible to fix ourselves without our Creator.

Scripture tells us, *"Nothing in all creation is hidden from God's sight."*—**Hebrews 4:13—NIV.**

There isn't a day or a tear that God does not know about. He sees whatever we are going through; He cares, and He knows. God longs to be known by you. He longs for you to make time to simply seek His face and get to know His personality, the nature of His love, and the availability of His presence. You don't have to live without a real, revelatory knowledge of God's heart. You don't have to live with the uncertainty of whether you are cared for, provided for, and loved.

Through the life, death, and resurrection of Jesus, God proved His longing to be known by us. Jesus took on flesh not just so He could save and redeem us, but so He could usher in a better, truer revelation of who the Father is.

John 17:3—NIV—Jesus says, *"Now this is eternal life: that they know you, the only true God, and Jesus Christ, whom you have sent."* And later in verse 26 Jesus prays to the Father, *"I have made you known to them, and will continue to make you known in order that the love you have for me may be in them and that I myself may be in them."* Jesus came that we might know the love of the Father. He came that we might have communion unhindered relationship with our Creator.

Through Jesus you have been granted eternal life, real access to your heavenly Father. And in the Holy Spirit you can search the deep places of God's heart and grow in restored relationship with him. **Paraphrased 1 Corinthians 2:10-12 KJV:**

"For the Spirit searches everything, even the depths of God. For who knows a person's thoughts except the spirit of that person, which is in him? So also no one comprehends the thoughts of God except the Spirit of God. Now we have received not the spirit of the world, but the Spirit who is from God, that we might understand the things freely given us by God."

God has made the way for you to know His heart. You can know Him in infinitely deeper and more transformative ways than you can know even your best friend or spouse. The Holy Spirit, God Himself, dwells within you and longs to reveal the deep things of Himself to you.

All that's left for you to do is have faith in God's ability to reveal Himself when you seek Him and set aside time to know the heart of your heavenly Father. Your will or choice is the most powerful tool you have along with your thoughts. This is so powerful because we have the choice to accept or reject God and His purpose for our lives. People are not what we think when our hearts are left unprotected, vulnerable to the snares of the enemy and unreachable by God.

A great self-evident truth for mankind, that God knows our hearts.

Secretly Miserable

The reason most of us are miserable is because we are living a lie. We all have our own way of hiding from our truth. We hide because it's painful, and we don't think we can change. Being secretly miserable is a result of unspoken thoughts caused by our perception affected by our emotions and feelings. When we begin to change our perception while controlling those thoughts our attitude on life will ultimately change those feelings of misery.

The issue is in your belief system, what you've heard about yourself, think about yourself or the constant voices in your head. The first step in changing your perception is knowing that you will become what you think. What you perceive can only be understood by relating it to what you have gone through. Introverts and intellectuals often hide behind labels and jargons. The givers of the world, the healers, mothers who are servers, can find it difficult to slow down enough to address their needs and desires.

People are not what you think when they are hurting internally; they are defensive and they lash out at others. As the saying goes, *"hurt-people hurt-people."* If they understood the power to change those thoughts of hurt, anger, and hatred, they would be transformed by the renewing of their minds.

"Don't become so well-adjusted to your culture that you fit into it without even thinking. Instead, fix your attention on God.

A Different Perspective

You'll be changed from the inside out. Readily recognize what he wants from you, and quickly respond to it. Unlike the culture around you, always dragging you down to its level of immaturity, God brings the best out of you, develops well-formed maturity in you."—**Romans 12:2**—MSG.

As our minds are being renewed, and we begin to draw closer to God, our desire to work with Him and not against Him allows change to occur. Change is never easy; it requires sacrifice and discipline. Never be satisfied with where you are because God always has more in store for you. Take the time to thank Him from the depths of your heart. *"Lord, I want to become what you say I can become. I am willing to accept whatever it takes for You to bring me there."*

Most of the time, when someone hurt me, I didn't allow myself to speak or think negatively about them. Instead, I made every effort to understand what would cause the individual to make their choices, even if I can't understand it.

Suppose you made a mistake; whether small or significant, the guilt and regrets can be overwhelming. The pain mixed with guilt, anger, and shame may take you time to release for healing. Maybe a prolonged illness or any deferred hope for something can bring on frustration. You are crying out for help with the belief that escaping from it is hopeless. I believe this is how depression starts and later may even evolve into premature death.

Forgiving yourself while being free from condemnation is the first path to happiness, good health, and acknowledging freedom from your pain and regrets. One day as I waited in

A Different Perspective

line at a store, I had a conversation with a young lady who confided in me that she didn't like herself. We were waiting for the attendant to come and fix the receipt tape for the woman in front of us while being the only two people in line. She believed life could have spared its ugly rod upon her instead of leaving her unhappy in her outlook on life.

I agreed with her and said, *"life does not always spare its ugly rod."* I explained that in order to move forward she must examine what happened, learn from it, and acknowledge if it's something she did to herself. Whatever the situation, *"what are you going to do with what's left of the pieces of your life?"*

We talked briefly, she left, and I never saw her again, but I did give her some simple instructions which I hope she followed. A few years later, I found myself in a similar situation, though I was supposed to be happy, nothing to complain about, but I wasn't happy.

After a second lay off or the industry term "reconstruction," roughly fifteen years ago, I was unemployed for almost a year. I was receiving unemployment, but it wasn't enough money to live on so I worked full time on temporary assignments. I later had to pay back some of the unemployment money received because I couldn't work temporarily and collect unemployment. If that wasn't bad, my years of experience worked against me because now companies don't want to pay me the same. Companies overqualified me, so they would not hire or pay more, thinking I would not stay longer than a year. I was frustrated but pushed my frustrations aside, so I pretended to handle it well without grieving my loss.

Of course, thinking about your feelings is not the same thing as feeling them. I hid from it for as long as possible until one day it all started spilling out in uncontrollable tears of overwhelming sadness. Just because everything in your life is running smoothly right now doesn't mean that it will last. In other words, life happens, and when it does, it completely turns your life upside down.

That experience taught me a lot about reinventing myself by adapting to change. First, I had to define myself. For instance, your title holds no value; it is what you did while holding the title that has value. Tell yourself you are valuable; you can reinvent yourself through your life and business experiences to be an asset, whether in corporate or as an entrepreneur.

Here is some Advice to Steer you Through the Process:

- Know what you want!
- Don't just understand what you don't want.
- Work toward something with the reinvention.
- Don't just run away from something else you can do.
- Get clear on what you want and why.
- Then when you get it, you will want what you have.
- Don't feel the need to justify your move.
- If someone is curious about your why, tell him or her in simple and truthful terms.
- No one can argue with the facts.

- People may have opinions, but the time they spend thinking about you is nothing like having to live your life 24 hours in a day.

- Find others — Get in touch with a reinvention mentor (life coach) or someone who has transitioned from profession to another. Such people are available more places than you would think and more people are wanting to reinvent themselves than ever before.

- Take action — Every day you spend in stagnation is one less day you'll spend in success. Small deliberate steps add up. Take one.

There are too many people looking at reinvention as a risk when it is an opportunity to learn and grow. Instead of asking yourself, what should I do, consider asking yourself, what do I want to get out of what it is that I do? This rephrasing illuminated a lot for me during my reinvention, and I hope it does for you, too. It is about getting what you want and more about enjoying what you get.

We are a culture of humans living in our heads and disconnected from our wisdom. In recent years we've become so consumed with happiness that we've lost connection to meaning. We prefer short-lived pleasure over deep healing. Instead of a thorough cleaning of a house, you settle for the surface, so it is partially clean. You want to receive complete healing of the spirit to carry throughout the entire body.

We don't want to feel uncomfortable, let alone process the deep emotional pain hidden in our beings. You might be grief-stricken, completely lost in life, depressed, and disillusioned. We all get there through different paths, but we all want the same things. Admit to yourself that you are sad and feel that you cannot enjoy anything or are lonely and afraid. There is hope in God, and He encourages us to call upon Him. The grace of God through Jesus is the sum of all hope.

"But thanks be to God, who gives us the victory through our Lord Jesus Christ."— **1 Corinthians 15:57.**

It's hard to separate our identity from what we pretend in a world that rewards flawless masks. The mask we wear might seem authentic, but they are just a disguise. Masks are tricky because they hide your identity, not your true self. In the early '20s, the Venetian Carnival encouraged mask use because it guaranteed total anonymity between the social classes. Masks allowed the lower-class people to be themselves and behave freely and equally. People could safely mock authority and aristocracy in public, but the intent to vent tensions and discontentment caused a surprising effect.

The wearing of masks permitted people to free their darkest side. Hiding one's identity became the perfect disguise for theft, freely committing robberies and physical attacks, and people's dark side left unchecked will arise in anger resulting in the unthinkable.

Individuals who do not have the ability to work with the full range of their feelings and conflicts often are handicapped in their development as a person. We induce physical symptoms on ourselves, such as headaches, gastrointestinal disorder, stress, and other physical symptoms. Often these same individuals may withdraw or even shut down at the first hint of anyone's anger.

Such withdrawal leads individuals to be taken advantage of, and it leaves them with only two options. They avoid all or most relationships to prevent being vulnerable, resulting in loneliness, isolation, and self-hatred. On the other hand, you can have a relationship with God and access Him whenever you need to; loneliness will become a thing of the past.

I hope we understand the need to stop hiding and pretending. For instance, hiding is working a job you have zero passion for and staying in toxic and lopsided romantic relationships or friendships. Building a life based on other people's definitions and wants for us, not our own. Over the years, this way of living will slowly begin to drown us, creating self-disconnection and deterioration.

Almost daily, we are asked the question, "How are you?" Did you know, "How are you" is a bland greeting for someone you haven't seen in a while? How are you doing is an actual inquiry about what is going on with someone. Maybe you knew the difference, but never really gave it much thought. Most people who ask, don't want to know the answer to either question.

Of course, we anticipate the usual answer of excellent or good. And the person responding doesn't tell the truth by saying he or she is okay. However, when someone asks a person in poor health, "How are you doing?" You are inquiring into the state of that person's health or medical recovery. It's easy for most people to pretend and smile than to burden another with their problem that no one would like to hear. These polite conversational questions are insincere filler greetings, and people know they are engaging in polite chit-chat.

When you ask, what usually follows is a lost opportunity and meaningless exchange without connecting with that person. Nevertheless, small talk can lead to a friendship or encouragement in helping that other person. Showing any little spark of concern from anyone can put a thought of hope into a person's unhappy life.

People are secretly hurting, afraid to speak about their shame, or too embarrass of how their lives have become. Did you know that most people working would rather be in a different job? When we feel sad or uncomfortable, it is our mind's way of telling us that we are out of balance. It means we are emotionally in pain, and we need time to heal. No one is ever totally continuously pleased because it's an unachievable hype!

The uncomfortable, but straightforward truth, is that everybody's mood fluctuates sometimes. We all have ups and downs with a wide range of emotions. Yes, you may have made some mistakes in the past that you need to resolve with yourself and others. Still, suppose your overall attitude towards yourself is one of constant criticism, seeing where you messed up rather than what you achieved. In that case, you are practically living in an abusive relationship with yourself, a relationship that makes you afraid to take any risks.

A Different Perspective

Let's Take a Look at Some of the Main Characteristics of a Toxic Person

1. Selfish — We've all been guilty of this one, but some people are defined by it. These are people who take and hardly ever give back. They don't care about your life and your priorities. Their primary concern and focus are on having their environment revolve around them.

2. Mean to other people — There are times when we don't handle a situation well, which paints us negatively. However, some people are just downright mean-spirited. You want to be around people who treat you with respect and decency. When you see someone, who is deliberately mean to people and can't communicate with him or her, you may want to leave them alone. Being kind can create meaningful relationships, and it also shows your true human nature.

3. Addicted to drama — Drama queens/kings thrive on negativity and drama. The primary strength of toxic people comes from bringing trouble into the life of other people. They see it all around them, they focus on this negativity, and they bring it with them everywhere they go.

4. Don't appreciate others — It's nice to be around people who enjoy you and appreciate the things you do for others. Some toxic people, on the other hand, want to demolish and to destroy a person. If you're around someone who is continually diminishing what you do and who you are, instead of appreciating you for who you are, then it's time to start looking at how you can reduce your exposure to them. The

emotional cost of having them around often far outweighs any benefits they might bring.

5. See themselves as the victim — Sure, bad things will happen during our lives, and we have to deal with them. But going through these difficult times, and playing the victim in every situation, are two different things. Toxic people tend to victimize themselves more often than not. This is the type of person you want to limit your exposure to. Eventually, they will find a way to point the finger at you for their behavior.

6. Constantly lying — So, no one is holier than thou. It's one thing to lie. It's quite another to lie to the point that people have learned not to trust you. You just have that feeling like you don't really believe them and they are probably lying. Well, then there's a good chance you're dealing with the pathological liar. They don't see the flaws within their personality either; instead, they focus on discrediting others, which can be an awful thing for you if you're associating with them.

7. Attention-seekers — Do you notice how some people are always in the middle of everything? Even if it has nothing to do with them, they want to get involved and get into the middle of the situation. Attention-seekers may or may not necessarily want chaos. They want all eyes on them; they want to be the center of attention. They crave and thrive on it.

Toxic people are mean to others to feel better about themselves because they are insecure with low self–esteem. These are people who don't see a problem or that the problem may be them.

One's Emotional State

- You don't know an individual's fragile emotional state standing beside you at a gas station, in the parking lot or wherever you go;

- That friendly neighbor that offered you sugar for your coffee because you were too lazy to go to the store;

- The lady that refuse to allow you to pull a mango that is hanging from her tree;

- The seemly good child that ran past you because he has stolen from the neighborhood store;

- That teacher who allowed his students disobedience to make him rise out of control in anger;

To feel happy, we must process the difficult things that happen and accept other emotions. I didn't say to launch out your anger because you are mad, but accept that feeling (anger) and learn how to channel it correctly.

Because we don't know one's fragile state, but if we all begin where we are to improve ourselves, each one will reach another. Extending kindness and compassion to others in our inner circle will spread like wildfire into our communities, cities, states, and abroad.

Let's look at Couples

If you ask couples married or in a dating relationship, some would admit having been in an unhappy relationship before. Good relationships are based on intentionality to talk and listen, facilitated by trust, commitment, and respect. Learning about each other is intentional, and the process is through communicating to realize compatibility and staying power.

The reality is who you both have to become to stay into a committed relationship while finding the proper balance for both. Marriage takes communication and listening, patience to continue working on yourself while encouraging your spouse, being in love, trust, etc. People who take their wedding vows seriously, who have been committed to faith and family, fall into trouble when they don't grow and change with their spouse throughout their marriage. We need to continually update our knowledge about our spouse.

For instance, how many times have you heard that a marriage has ended because one spouse had an affair and the other spouse was oblivious? Everyone thought they were the perfect couple, and no one saw that coming. The spouse committing the infidelity isn't the way you think he or she is. What's beneath the spouse's surface has masquerade and manifested into an affair onto the other spouse.

Weekly, for an hour, set aside time, not for the business of home, but to talk about each person's feelings and thoughts. Like a yearly physical with your doctor instead of a weekly one with your spouse. Maybe, it is why date night is a common practice to get married couples to reconnect.

Here are my results through communicating with people who have unfortunately experienced divorce through infidelity.

- People have affairs not because they are looking for another person, but because they desire another version of themselves.

- It's not the spouse they seek to leave with the affair; it's themselves.

- It's a part of themselves that they don't like, which they have been out of touch with for years.

- An affair is a rebellion against oneself in the relationship.

- Often, affairs are initiated by a spouse as an exit strategy, which can result in a divorce or a separation.

- The aftermath of an affair is that both spouses are in crisis, not just the spouse who cheated.

The tendency is to leave or divorce, and even though I agree, there are legal grounds because trust and covenant have been broken. Every person or situation is different; there might be a chance the relationship can survive the affair if they analyze the blind spots that surround the infidelity.

By their consent, the man and woman enter into this agreement with God at the center of their relationship. It is meant to be held in honor as the most intimate human relationship, sacred; a gift from God. Marriage between a man and a woman is ordained of God, but not every marriage is God ordained.

However, both partners must be willing to address the issues and work on their survival for a stronger, healthier, and happier relationship. Whatever the result of the marriage after infidelity, forgiveness is imperative for one's wholeness and growth. Forgiveness is for you and not the other person;

un-forgiveness will destroy your peace and prevent you from moving forward into real purpose.

This is why we are miserable because we live in our humanity without consulting our creator, the all-knowing one. He has established that both whole (complete) and committed individuals with His wisdom should enter into a relationship to create a successful marriage. **—Genesis 2:18-19—** *And the Lord God said, "It is not good that man should be alone, I will make him a helper comparable to him."* However, if you have already married without God's blessings, seek His wisdom for wherever you are in this relationship.

Socially Connected

People are like a puzzle by trying to connect each piece with the right insight. You begin to understand each component in such a way to see the intention. The idea is that every detail in the puzzle no matter how obscure the piece is designed to fit. If a piece is missing it must be found because there can't be any open spaces. Not every piece is the same because everyone is uniquely different but all the pieces work as a component to create God's beautiful picture of a shared humanity. The challenge is for us to recognize everyone's significance while learning to celebrate our differences as we join together in piecing our purpose to complete the puzzle.

If we accept this challenge, we must first know we are similar for having thoughts but differ in belief in the fervent power of our thoughts. Recognize the key to understanding human behavior is to understand the needs that drive us. The first need is to acknowledge our dependency on God for wisdom to know how to connect socially.

We take our basic human needs and come up with rules for how we're going to respond in certain situations, and develop them into cognitive feats, problematic behaviors, and interactions. Humankind is considered a social being who interact with other humans while getting to know each other and building meaningful relationships. It's about building genuine relationships and also about building robust support systems with other people in the form of friends, family, and colleagues.

The goal is to connect with good moral people who will draw out a Godly character. Saying that humans are a social being is usually followed by explaining why we need to do something together or why you should not be alone. In America, there are a vast amount of people from different countries, who speak other languages and have different skin tones. Life is supposed to be living harmoniously with everyone.

An easy beautiful concept, but too complicated for some to comprehend who believes different skin tones should not be social beings together. We find it easier to outcast groups of people before we decide to love them for who they are and for their differences. We are all the same, humans, we have skin, lungs, feet, hands and teeth. So, what makes us so different?

For example, if you have a neighborhood group that regularly meets at each other's homes, everyone could get to know all the people who live behind fences and closed doors. The neighbors would agree on some social activities that all could take part in. Most of the neighbors are fine with it, but there will be a few people who don't want to be part of the group or any of its activities. Sadly, they decide to set themselves apart because they are private people. However, the others struggle to understand when they had all reached out to them and found it problematic that some amongst us are anti-social.

Maybe, they were hurt from past relationships, have restraints on their time, or never learned how to celebrate or appreciate the gift of building good connections. We all love to have people around us to support us when we are facing dire times in our lives, and we also love to share our happiness with others. Respect people, and build your social group where you can share stuff, help each other or ask for help from them. God did not create humans as a solitary being; He wanted us to be sociable.

We are most comfortable when connected, sharing strong emotions, stories, and cooperating to achieve something in common. We are biologically, cognitively, physically, and spiritually wired to love, be loved, and belong. When those needs are not met, we don't function as we were meant to. We may think we want money, power, fame, beauty, eternal youth or a new car. But at the root of most of these desires is a need to belong, be accepted, connect with others and be loved.

We pride ourselves on our independence, pulling ourselves up by our bootstraps, having a successful career and not depending on anyone. Social connection is also essential to improve physical health and one's psychological well-being. Socially connecting is vital as a whole, but let's examine the emotional side related to men versus women. Contrary to a famous saying, "*a true man shows emotions and expresses his feelings.*"

Boys are taught as early as elementary school that they are sissies if they show fear, pain, or emotions like crying. Girls have the licenses to continue a full range of emotional

101

expressions, except for anger. Girls get angry, of course, but it is taboo for us to express it. It is not feminine to get or express anger, which has caused women a world of grief into their adult lives. Ironically, anger is one of the few acceptable emotions sanctioned for boys to express publicly. Let's look at emotions or most people I have heard say feelings.

They are very much the same naturally we would perceive them as synonyms. However, even though they are dependent on each other, emotions and feelings are somewhat different things. Emotions describe physiological states and are generated subconsciously. Usually, they have the freedom to govern themselves or control their bodily responses to certain external or internal events. By contrast, feelings are subjective experiences of emotions and are driven by conscious thoughts and reflections. This means that we can have emotions without having feelings. However, we cannot have feelings without having emotions. This is why people lose it because their feelings are triggered by emotions, and they become unrecognizable. Feelings are a learned behavior resulting from our emotions, if not guided by reasoning or the Spirit of God, over time, can be explosive.

Seemly, if we are operating out of our negative feelings (danger zone) how do we still interact with society, and society does not fully understand it. I question how people's interactions can create the illusion of a shared social order despite not fully understanding each other. I get it, one or maybe two people could slip away through the cracks, but one life is too precious to lose. There is a problem with us as social beings if someone, in our schools, our work environments, friends, nor family, cannot decipher a problem in someone's life.

Have we forgotten the good shepherd's mindset who leaves the 99 to get the one lost sheep? Conscious or unconsciously, we control information to and in our social interactions. In other words, I hold your perception of me, socially, we maintain our perception of each other and the world. If you have not spotted it yet, the root word here is perception. Perception, as defined by Google, *"a way of regarding, understanding, or interpreting something; a mental impression."*

Here's another definition for perception: Organizational Behavior — Perception.

"Perception is an intellectual process of transforming sensory stimuli to meaningful information. It is the process of interpreting something that we see or hear in our mind and use it later to judge and give a verdict on a situation, person, group etc."[2]

By now, you are getting an understanding of why people we associate with often or in passing may not be what we think. Based on your perception of your reality in a social environment, you may develop deeply rooted fears of rejection. We desire to be sociable, but sometimes, anxiety holds us from being who we are because of fear of acceptance.

---

[2] www.bing.com/search?q=organizational+behavior+perception+google&cvid

Here are some situations; the fear of rejection can cause people to act differently socially.

The fear of rejection is a powerful fear that has a broad impact on our lives. Most people experience some nerves when placing themselves in situations that could lead to rejection, but for some people, it's crippling. An untreated fear of rejection tends to worsen over time, gradually taking over every part of your life.

Even something as simple as answering the telephone can be terrifying for those suffering from a fear of rejection and picking up the phone to call someone.

Dating — Is overwhelming if you suffer from a fear of rejection. Rather than focusing on getting to know the other person and deciding whether you would like a second date, you might spend all of your time worrying whether that person likes you. Obsessive worrying, a visibly nervous demeanor, trouble speaking are everyday things.

Marriage — No matter how compatible you maybe, two people can't agree on everything. Those with a fear of rejection often have difficulty expressing their own needs and standing their ground. You might also develop feelings of jealousy or distrust in your partner as your fear of rejection turns into a fear of being abandoned and expressed in such unhealthy behaviors as checking your partner's phone messages or social media accounts.

Meeting New People — We are social creatures, and we are expected to follow basic social rules in public. Most of the time, idle chatter in the grocery line or the elevator lasts only a few moments. Occasionally, short conversations can lead to lifelong friendships. If you fear rejection, you may feel unable to chat with strangers or even friends of friends. The tendency to keep to yourself could potentially prevent you from making lasting connections with others.

Peer Pressure — The need to belong is essentially a human condition. We tend to select, cheerleaders, nerds, clubs, or any number of other small groups in high school. As adults, we tend to organize by shared interests, relationship status, and such. If your fear of rejection leads you to do things that are illegal, immoral or merely distasteful to you, then peer pressure might be a problem in your life.

Phoniness — Fearing that you will be rejected if you show your true self to the world, you may live life behind a mask. The fear of rejection will make you seem phony and not authentic to others and may cause an unwillingness to embrace life's challenges.

People-Pleasing — Although it is natural to want to take care of those we love, those who fear rejection often go too far. You might find it impossible to say no, even when saying yes causes major inconveniences or hardships in your own life. You may take on too much, increasing your own risk for burnout. At the extreme, people-pleasing sometimes turns into enabling the destructive behaviors of others. Worried that you will lose the other person, you might make excuses or even assist the person with actions you know are wrong.

Unassertiveness — People with a fear of rejection often go out of their way to avoid confrontations. You might refuse to ask for what you want or even speak up for what you need. A common tendency is to shut down your own needs or pretend that they don't matter.

Passive-Aggressiveness — Uncomfortable showing off their true selves but unable to entirely shut out their own needs, many people who fear rejection end up behaving in passive-aggressive ways. You might procrastinate, forget to keep promises, complain, and work inefficiently on whatever you take on.

The fear of rejection often stops us from going after our dreams. Putting yourself out there is frightening for anyone, but you may feel paralyzed if you have a fear of rejection. Hanging onto the status quo feels safe, even if you are not happy with your current situation. Whether you want to travel the world, write the great American novel, the fear of rejection may stop you from reaching your full potential.

Reactions of Others — The fear of rejection leads to behaviors that make us appear insecure, ineffectual, and overwhelmed. You might sweat, shake, avoid eye contact, and even lose the ability to communicate effectively. While individuals react to these behaviors in very different ways, these are some of the reactions you might see.

Rejection — It is well known that confidence enhances attractiveness. As a general rule, the lack of self-confidence, inherent in a fear of rejection makes us more likely to be rejected.

Manipulation — Some people prey on the insecurities of others. Those who suffer from a fear of rejection may be at greater risk of being manipulated for someone else's gain. Expert manipulators generally come across as charming, sophisticated, and genuinely caring; they know what buttons to push to make others trust them. They also know how to keep someone with a fear of rejection feeling slightly on edge as if the manipulator might leave. Almost always, the manipulator does end up going once he has gotten what he wants out of the other person.

Frustration — Most people in the world are decent, honest and forthright. Rather than manipulating someone with a fear of rejection, they will try to help. Look for signs that your friends and family are trying to encourage your assertiveness, asking you to be more open with them, or probing your true feelings. However, many times, people who fear rejection see these attempts to help as signs of possible future rejection. This fear of rejection often leads friends and family to walk on eggshells, fearful of making your fears worse. Over time, they may become frustrated and angry, either confronting you about your behavior or beginning to distance themselves from you.

By improving your self-esteem and self-confidence, you can overcome a fear of rejection. Now that you have a better understanding of what your fear of rejection looks like, you're ready to handle it. Working out how to handle rejection and how to improve self-esteem are gradual processes that are slightly different for everyone. However, whether you're looking to learn how to deal with rejection from friends, deal with rejection in love, or how to handle rejection from a job, the key steps are the same.

Step 1 — When you hold on to the false assumption that others will always reject you, you create situations where rejection occurs. Start fighting this by deliberately looking for signs of acceptance and write them down if it helps.

Step 2 — Focus on how you want to be, for example, making it a goal to make friends at school or get a promotion at work by next year.

Step 3 — When learning how to improve self-confidence, it's essential to know where the lack began. Who taught you to fear rejection? Where did you receive messages suggesting you lack value? These limiting beliefs often come from things that happened when you were young. Once you make them concrete, you can challenge them, and they start to lose their power.

Step 4 — Overcoming the fear of rejection makes creative use of the imagination. Every day make time to visualize yourself acting confidently in situations that generally make you feel insecure. Imagine yourself not only surviving but thriving, unworried by the idea of rejection. In time, this visual habit can help to reshape your thoughts and expectations.

Step 5 — When you embrace not being rejected, it often leads to feeling certain that you will not be rejected again.

Step 6 — Getting over rejection also requires that you learn to see it differently. You can survive the end of a relationship, or a job that doesn't work out, or a friendship that no longer fits when you catch yourself fretting over what-if questions, challenge yourself to imagine how you would overcome the scenario and find happiness again.

Step 7 — Finally, everyone, all your favorite musicians, actors, family, friends, have experienced rejection. When you get rejected, you probably assume it means something awful about you. But how do you feel about others who have experienced rejection?

Try to see that experiencing rejection isn't the same as unlovable, worthless or destined to be alone. In other words, rejection doesn't have to carry that much weight unless you let it. Our defensive structure not only safeguards us from possible rejection, but also from the prospect of being accepted and welcomed. There is a corresponding fear that is less visible, a fear of being accepted.

Being Accepted Can Be Frightening — There can be scary implications for being accepted. You meet someone at a social event who likes you. This person asks for your phone number. What now? Are you flooded with fear? What if this person begins to see who you are? What might they see? What if they don't like you? And what if they seem to like you?

We have blockage to receiving — You may not know what to do with compliments or positive attention. You might shut down so that you don't have to let down your defenses and expose yourself. And what if they no longer accept you at some point? That might hurt! So, you play it safe by distancing as a preemptive defense against possible future pain.

We cling to core negative beliefs — When someone likes or accepts us, then negative core beliefs might be up for review. If we believe that we're unlovable or that relationships always fail, we might not know how to respond when evidence contradicts our core belief.

We have an avoidance or indecisive attachment — The fear of acceptance may be operating if we tend to avoid relationships. In addition to fearing rejection, we might keep distant because we don't trust that any incipient connection or acceptance will last. If we're unsure about relationships, some part of us wants connection, and another part is frightened by if we might yield to our fear and pull away at the first sign of discord.

Overcoming the fear of acceptance may mean exploring blockage to receiving and examining core beliefs that keep us stuck. This acceptance might involve a radical change in our self-image. Viewing ourselves more positively, and our potential to love and be loved means that our life might change. Change can be scary. Change or the lack of it is another reason why people are not what you think.

We know what we need to do, but doing it is an act of our will. We may turn to people we trust, pastors, people of faith, psychologists, to help us see ourselves right. First, we must pray, seek God's help for a revelation of self-image to envision what is wrong with us and to make the necessary adjustments.

Unless God heals us in our broken areas, we will not live and grow into the people that He Created us to be. I don't mean religion because nowhere in scripture has God ordained an institution. He speaks about a personal relationship with God through His Son. Religion is human-made; I'm not against it, as long as the central focus is on a real love relationship with God and everyone else.

Inner healing is needed whenever we become aware that we are held down in any way by the hurts of the past or present. The term healing is biblical, but the term inner healing isn't found anywhere in scriptures. There might be other meanings, but I'll use it as such. Not all methods that people use are biblical. Some techniques that people use are rooted more in secular psychology, spiritualism, or even the occult.

Although I would have to say that some non-believing psychologists can offer useful insights as long as it is rooted in love with a genuine need to help others, this is still God at work through the non-believer.

Inner healing is the process of inviting Jesus to heal your innermost parts that were damaged through life experiences.

We are all sinners as the bible said, *"All have sinned and come short of the glory of God."*—**Romans 3:23**—KJV.

People can receive help through prayer counseling, where they are encouraged to do the following things:

- Confess you are a sinner in need of a Savior (Jesus).
- Forgive the ones who have wronged you.
- Repent of your sins and receive healing from your brokenness.
- Release your hurts, your brokenness and deepest heart wounds.

- Allow the Spirit of God to deliver you from the power of your brokenness and sins.

When we are not whole from within, we don't see ourselves truthfully and accept limitations and areas of personal excellence. Wholeness in a person can integrate (through Christ) both good and bad as part of reality. The book of **Romans Chapter 6** is significant in this regard to the power we have in our everyday life to live in faithful ways to God.

Humbly facing the truth, God will work by His Spirit and bring cleansing and a transformation into your life. Often, beautiful, emotional healing is the result. The intent of humanity is much more than to co-exist. We get to know and see people as real people; it is us becoming the gift and lovingly serving one another. You see people for who they are and what they can add to your life and what you can add to theirs.

For everyone in our communities to rise out of the fear of acceptance and rejection, becoming a healthy society, will depend on its men and women's interior growth. Where each individual can aspire to fulfill their potential without the crippling effects that fear and hurt produce.

Media

E veryone's unique story began at birth with genes, DNA, specific traits, and our own experiences. As a media production with lights, cameras, family, and friends, they are waiting for your life to begin. Maybe you don't believe you were an excellent thought in God's head. Your uniqueness is why you are here to fulfill His amazing thought and plan for your life.

Your chances to be born were slim as sperm cells fought to attach itself to an egg, and yet, you are here! As life happens and so we individually perceive and interpret it our way. Still, at any given time, what we think is based solely on whatever is going on in our internal movie screen in our heads. Our customized movie is drawn-out and personal. Your movie is very different from someone else because everyone is different. While everyone's movie is unique, we, the observers, are the same stuff. Unlike the rating G, R, or PG of a movie, your movie won't make sense to anyone viewing it except you.

You will be shocked if you could somehow get hold of someone's movie in their head. However, if our movies were revealed, what is playing would be the real us simultaneously—our true selves behind our stories and the blank slate babies we were born to be. The beautiful souls underneath our fears and the perfect pieces of our potential are our true nature.

113

Imagine a mirror of mutual knowledge easily accessible about us all, depicted on a screen for everyone to see what we are. Wow, can you really envision this in this already digital world? It's hard to think of all the implications of a no secret safe society.

If our lives were so transparent, it should motivate us to become a better version of ourselves. Will it show our true humanity that paradoxes sometimes contradict being a good neighbor besides the tendency to walk away seeing our neighbor in need? What does it mean to be human? Perhaps we only begin to answer this when we turn to the one who shows us its very meaning.

The goal of media is to inform us of whatever is newsworthy by entertaining, educating, and to keep us coming back for more of the same. Media influence controls the message; the quality is interpreted through radio, tv, movie, social media, etc. Like an interpreter who stands between to relay the news or what is being communicated to another. However, the interpreter must be able to understand and share the message with accuracy.

Let's View Media Effects on Us

The news media is an umbrella for all the news sources to include newspapers, television, radio, printed matter, internet information, and advertising. With all of the information sources available to us, people have own up to being stressed, suffering anxiety, fatigue, and sleep loss. Most people are overloaded with social media but compete to stay informed with the likes on Facebook and other social media.

Even media outlets have responded to Americans' increasing dependence on television and the internet by making the news even more readily available. I think the problem is being too readily accessible is making some people overloaded. Over the past two years, I became aware of our media issues from co-workers and strangers I met in stores while shopping.

Over the last 15 years, I have seen changes in how our news is presented and how information is accessed. In conversations with my peers because the news focuses primarily on negative happenings, i.e. crime, murder, violence, people can now access and view the news 24/7 on their cell phones, tablets, laptops, and car radios while out and about. And if they are home, it's viewed on their TV.

People still feel it necessary to stay informed. There are pros and cons to everything in life, and that includes social media. Based on what I've heard while interacting with others, let's examine what heavy social media is doing to most people.

As you go through them, ask yourself how you can take advantage of the pros while minimizing the cons whenever you decide to check out your favorite social media.

- The reality is that people connecting with people has proven health benefits.
- You can find a large amount of health-related information on social media, which is quite helpful. On the other hand, if you take random advice without doing proper research, it can also be harmful.

- There are helpful tips in general on social media.

- Instagram has helped many restaurants reach their customers and hear their opinions and experiences. I believe a picture is worth a thousand words, and Instagram has proven that.

- With that said, we are overeating because posted food photos on social media have increased our appetites.

- People without self-control are spending more money because of compelling advertisement.

- Social media has damaged real live conversation due to a lack of immediate involvement resulting in social withdrawal from each other. Millennials often hide behind computers and speak their mind through Twitter and blogs. They don't place value in face-to-face communication. On the other hand, Boomers like to talk to someone in person.

- With the lack of involvement, it leads to increased feelings of depression, anxiety, poor body image and loneliness.

- No wonder why some of our teens and adults suffer from drug, alcohol, low self-esteem, obesity, and mental issues.

In speaking with 50 adults in varying age groups, I found that most people check the news every hour or throughout the day and are constantly monitoring social media, which often exposes them to the latest news headlines, whether they like it or not. Then there were twelve out of the 50 people I spoke with who didn't care for social media.

We like to think that we are logical and that when we are making a decision, we carefully weigh all of our alternatives. Even when people think they are making a conscious, rational decision, the chances are that they aren't aware that they have already decided and that it was unconscious. We aren't even aware of our process. Nor are we aware that we make decisions based on logic and our emotions.

It would be best if you assumed that all decisions involve emotions. You are more likely to persuade people to take any action if you understand how they feel about the decision and feed their feelings. Basically, this is what media has done in marketing by advertising to focus on our decision-making feelings. If we are not careful, the media will tell us what to do so we don't think anymore.

When I see news stories where people are caught doing dreadful acts with children, I have to step back and tell myself, "I don't have all the facts yet." I want to believe that they caught the bad guys. And in most cases, especially in child abuse of any sort, the bad guys have been caught. Because there are so few people who turn out to be good in these cases, the ones who are truly innocent end up suffering and going through the process until they are cleared. And even then, they are never cleared because there are still people out there that believe the person is guilty.

We have trouble reconciling the fact that someone is lying with what we perceive as expressions of honesty. Denial of reality, or not accepting something that we know is true in some part of our brain, is how we unconsciously protect ourselves from pain. With denial, we can assure ourselves that everything is okay, even when it is not. However, we cannot solve a problem we don't acknowledge.

Again, media play with our feelings, but before we imprison someone in our heads, let's get all the facts. We are also so socially concerned and obsessed with media and about our favorite celebrities. It's disturbing to think of suicide by a star because of their wealth, facilitating any available resources. Remember the beloved food critic who took us worldwide to explore how food and culture can bring us together. His death and many famous people we admired, were unfortunately not what we thought they were.

Their talents drew us close to them, but not close enough to understand their true identity or struggles. When you are a public figure, there's a lot of pressure. When your status is one of stardom, your surroundings are rarely by genuine and caring people. People are usually looking for an opportunity for themselves through you. Whatever knowledge one might have about a celebrity is impersonal information. We don't have personal experience with a star unless we know them personally through interaction.

Fame represents something that we want and think we can attain by becoming famous. Media has confirmed what we already knew that public recognition brings its own problems and that those who have it are not any happier or better off than others. The fact is that being in the public eye is a mixed blessing; however, being famous isn't all that bad if you are remembered for being a gorgeous woman or man of your time.

When you are a celebrity or superstar in today's culture, everybody cares and wants a piece of you; you're the face everybody wants to see. Your every word and action counts;

the pressure is on. But make a wrong decision or say something stupid, and you're labeled for life. Just as fast as you were elevated is the same speed, if not faster, that the same people will want to see you suddenly come down.

Being wealthy or famous doesn't count; it's happy and content with oneself. Unfortunately, everyone you know may not be because we are all at different places on our journeys. However, what is newsworthy to a certain extent can ignite fear. Through social media and such, we can be socially connected worldwide but have anxiety about crime, murder, discrimination, and our financial status. Then there are those with issues within themselves who will not seek help due to low self-esteem, fear of rejection, acceptance, etc.

In an attempt to continue to evolve personally, spiritually, and professionally it's necessary to break from all news media and focus on wholesome experiences. Enjoy the simple pleasures of life, swimming, and sports, whatever your skills, hobbies, or talents are. Spending quality time with families and friends while staying focus on positive social interactions to stay connected.

The Bible is the ultimate source for truth, and God is faithful to fulfill all His promises. As you read the below promises, claim them over your life:

- Freedom from addictions;
- Deliverance from sin and all manner of evil;
- Financial provision;

- Hope for the lost;

- Hurting family and friends;

- Overcoming depression;

- Recovering a marriage;

- Good health and healing;

- Freedom from fear and anxiety;

- Walking in authority and power.

These are just a few; there are many more blessings and gifts that God promises to provide for those who believe in Him. And because of this, our faith is imperative because it is a reminder of God's unconditional love; and the Word-filled with promises from our Creator to provide, deliver, and protect us. Notice I did not say religion or being religious, but merely childlike faith in God that leads to a relationship and not religion.

God intends to have a personal relationship with you through your life's journey. God is the inner healer available to you and me or anyone who desires to receive His invitation. In fact, in our thought process, there is something in our subconscious (like an auto-pilot) needing re-programming to reinforce the wholesome image of ourselves. We don't have to conform to what media offers, let's create positive, inspiring movies, love songs, etc.

Your subconscious mind is like the auto-pilot feature on a remote control or airplane. It has been pre-programmed to follow a specific route, and you can't deviate from that course unless you change the direction programmed into it. In contrast, Christ is the one who makes our resuscitation possible and the one who restores in us the image of God.

Don't get me wrong, the news media isn't all bad, everything has its place, but spend time with God first to find the proper use and the enjoyment of all the world's media. Through the Bible and many different translations, God's word has stood the test of time as the infallible printed, audible message of love and redemption to all humanity.

Get It Together

For most of us, getting our lives together is more of a state of mind or possibly a conviction. If truth be told, we know it when we feel it. There are moments when we think we have gotten the hang of life, but are we playing a game in which we are unaware of the rules.

For instance, your free choice means life is ready to respond to your thoughts. We feel flawed because our inability to get ourselves together for long seems impossible. So, we use this notion that we can or should be perfect as an excuse to dislike ourselves. The reality is everyone has felt this way, but some people live in this mindset of fear. Don't surrender to being desperate because of fear, but seek environments to bring about faith and hope.

For some people, having their life together means happily married with kids, mortgage paid off, and financially secure. It's paying your bills and getting laundry done, for some, it means passing out drunk; less than three times a week. It's that Sunday when your house is clean, plans made, face mask on, etc. Most of us are suffering from life on broken pieces meaning we are still trying to get ourselves and our lives together.

Children don't have themselves together, and as adults, we can't stumble through the world playing and having fun. Childhood ends, and we find ourselves as adults in a world

123

where we are not and can never be enough. Suddenly, we cannot do as we wish; we must start life by undoing everything we learned about the world in childhood. We discovered so much of what we don't like about life. We get it; it's really about growing up and becoming an adult.

Adulthood is hard at first because we are responsible for ourselves. You are no longer allowed to play all day, sleep when you wish, pout, and have others give in. Being a child, we get to experience the joy of the moment because adults let us be in a state where we are enough. In childhood, we are completely loved, adored, held, cuddled, attended, and responded to. Children have thoughts about only sleeping, eating, and playing because these are their truly satisfying pleasures.

Adults have different pleasures like drinking because it makes us feel good, things like living on the edge, sports, and sex as a temporary fix to our problems. It's time to understand what we are afraid of and not let that ruin our lives. Stop being afraid of being an adult and take responsibility for yourself. You can't go back to childhood, where you had no duties because everything was taken care of for you.

Ever observe a young family out at dinner; they allow the younger kids iPads to keep them quiet. There is a minimum, if any, conversation, and most millennials cannot anticipate time management while shocked to discover the car needs gas, dry cleaning must be picked up, and there is no food in the pantry. They would prefer sitting with the iPad's and smartphones rather than paying attention to what needs to be done. Some millennials do not understand how to juggle life's responsibilities that everyone has to think. Instead, they are occupied with Facebook, Twitter, Instagram, and such because they live in a computer society where they don't have to think.

Being an adult means we figure out what matters, what we should focus our energy on, and what we should let go. Don't let fear set in, so we compromise and don't change our mindset. Keep in mind, *"I can do all things through Christ, which strengthens me."* —**Philippians 4:13**—KJV.

We can find Christ's strength through every season good or bad, through loss, promotions, school, pregnancy, child-rearing, marriage, employment, friendships, etc. The idea of getting yourself together is different from everyone, but it's usually a combination of being stable financially, mentally, socially, spiritually, and physically.

When we discipline our thoughts and accurately label them, our feelings can help us cope more effectively. Watch what you say because your words will transform into actions building your habits and forming your character. If you discipline your thought process, you will begin to see yourself more committed to start that business, completing those three credits for that degree, even committing to a marriage relationship.

In **Romans 2:4—(paraphrased)**, the goodness of God will lead you to Him, to rest in Him and to trust Him. However, you have to know that God is good. Dr. Myles Monroe said, *"Where* *purpose is not known abuse is inevitable."* Everything has a purpose, but not all-purpose is known, and when the goal is not known, the abuse is inevitable. Abuse derives from the words abnormal use. In other words, when you don't understand why something exists then you will abuse it because it is not being utilized or consumed in the way it was designed.

No designer ever begins with the design, they always have a purpose, and the plan is to fulfill that intent. Purpose resides in the manufacturer or the designer, so if you want to find an item's purpose, then you ask the manufacturer. It's the manufacturer who made the machine that knows why he made it. Human beings are the only creature God has problems with because we test His plan. In the same way, we must obey the instructions of the manufacturer of a thing to ensure success. It is the same way we must abide by God's laws and design for our lives for our protection to guarantee success.

Suppose we define purpose as the original intent for creating anything and the desired result that made the creation necessary. In that case, it suffices to say that this original intent is not in the product but the producer's mind. We are the original intent of our Creator God, so if we need to know our purpose, let's find out from God's mind. When men do not see the purpose of their spouse, they abuse them as punching bags.

Have you found your purpose, or are you abusing your life? For every abuse, there is a good expected use. Have you found your good use of whatever gifts, talents, and skills you have? Most of us are not honest with ourselves, so we become frustrated with our lives because we do not know our purpose. If there is no purpose, there is no structure in life, and the lack of structure leads to decisions that are not fully formed with a central goal. Thus, leading to poor and erratic choices like addictions. While accepting others' mistakes is part of letting go of the past and viewing others with compassion, this is more about you carrying your own mistakes, not feeling haunted by regrets, and afraid to move forward in your life.

2 Timothy 1:7—KJV says, *"God has not given us the spirit of fear; but of power, and of love, and of a sound mind."*

Creating a more positive outlook can lead to better outcomes. That's not to say positive thoughts have powers, but optimistic thoughts lead to productive behavior, which increases your chances of a successful outcome. Challenge your conclusions to take a look at the labels you have placed on yourself. Maybe you've declared yourself incompetent. Or perhaps you've decided you're a terrible person or leader. Remind yourself that you don't have to allow those beliefs to restrict your potential just because you think something doesn't make it right.

The good news is, you can change how you think. You can alter your perception and change your life. Here are two ways to challenge your beliefs:

Think of times when your beliefs weren't reinforced and acknowledge exceptions to the rule will remind you that your belief isn't always true. Challenge your ideas, perform behavioral experiments that test how accurate your thoughts are. If you think you're not good enough, do something that helps you to feel worthy. If you've labeled yourself too wimpy to step outside of your comfort zone, force yourself to do something that feels a little uncomfortable.

With practice, you can train your brain to think differently. When you give up those self-limiting beliefs, you'll be better equipped to reach your most significant potential. Define what you want in life. Know where you are going and arm yourself with a well-designed plan on how to get there. If you don't know where to start, begin with the missing things from your life. What will give purpose and meaning to your existence?

Get curious about the things you can achieve and how much more you can accomplish. Remind yourself that, at the end of life, the most important thing for a human being is the legacy they leave behind. Get it together by perceiving what you have accomplished with an excellent positive attitude, get your life in order and then regularly analyze your development growth.

You Are More Than That

Our thoughts and beliefs are so much more than just perceptions; they are physical energy as real as someone's embrace. They are the primary creative forces in revealing the life we currently have. How we think affects everything from our ability to solve problems to how we understand the meaning, value, and purpose.

Your success is determined not by what happens in society, but by what happens in your home, thoughts, and development over time. The objective is to become what you are capable of being rather than settling for what you are. Why settle for what you are rather than becoming what you can be?

We don't recognize people who have fallen away from society into homelessness or hopelessness because they have given up on life and stop becoming. We can't even begin to imagine what kind of thoughts they have allowed living within their mindset. If we become hopeless, understanding this hopelessness mindset means living without faith in despair and beneath your potential.

Whereas becoming is a matter of growing into oneself, perhaps the way a caterpillar becomes a butterfly or a seed becomes a plant. In a sense, it already is what it will become, but in another sense, it is not yet that thing. Specifically, the challenge is to change by you acting upon it.

To become who you are is to rise yet again as something new and different to transform. Becoming is the ongoing process of evolving, expressing yourself in a new way, yet still physically being the same person. Don't run from what happened to you or live in shame about negative things in your life. You have to face yourself and use what happened to you to become who you are to become. Know who God created you to be, especially in the dark times of life when you became broken, unsure of yourselves, faced rejection, lost hope, or forgot all that you have within you to become.

What you are going to be is hidden in who you are and what you were. There is a term where the loser is called the underdog, and the winner the top dog. In the natural, the person considered as the underdog begins to change his thoughts and sees himself as a winner. Although others didn't expect him to win, he becomes an overcomer to defeat the obstacle that has kept him defeated.

I love this quote from the movie The Lion King, *"Look inside yourself; you are more than what you have become."* In this movie, Simba had to remind himself who he was before moving forward to becoming. Becoming more is different than having or doing more because it's easier to measure doing than being.

Perhaps We are All a Work in Progress

Do you have a book, play, or movie stuck inside of you? Everyone has information, a skill, a gift, and abilities inside of them that needs to come out. Whether it's an unwritten book, play, movie, a speech, it starts within a thought.

The plan is to get out of the closet by gathering your thoughts by putting those journal ideas together as you develop your craft. There is so much more inside of you, anticipating its emergence outside of your body. Writing a book, script, or play takes a lot of work. But anything worth achieving takes effort, which is part of the challenge.

I believe God's plan is for us to stretch and grow as we progress. That's a much better option for you than putting it off and feeling unfulfilled. You naturally feel overwhelmed because your mental picture of that book, play, or movie is too big. Start with a blog, create an audience, but whatever you do, develop it, finish the book, and get it published.

One of the most important things in life is discovering God's purpose in our lives and using our talents to make the world a better place; we all have that power within us. We all can change the world and bring joy to the people in our lives. God has imparted gifts to each of us, and we need to use those gifts to bring happiness to ourselves and others. We should all make the most of the talents and gifts we have, and we should never think that what we have is insignificant. If it came from God; it's Good!

Becoming who you are to become does not mean that you have reached a height where no more change is needed. You must always be in the process of becoming until you have fulfilled everything you were born to do, create, and accomplish in your life. Have faith in the manifestation also mean you will have made room for growth. Here is something

131

you probably already knew, but quite possibly have forgotten along the way.

Maybe recent life events have occurred that have caused you to question your faith and your value or significance. Perhaps you feel like you have made some huge mistakes that have permanently put you out of reach from God's love, forgiveness, and grace. The guilt, shame, and anxiety have been destroying you emotionally and spiritually. The enemy has deceived you into believing some untrue things about yourself that have robbed you of your hope and joy in the Lord.

If that is you, or someone you know, these powerful lyrics to this song titled *"You are More"* will encourage you. Here is the Chorus:

"You are more than the choices that you've made,

You are more than the sum of your past mistakes,

You are more than the problems you create; you've been remade." ~ Tenth Avenue North.

God is repairing His people. You may have heard or read the story in the Bible when satan came to Eve in the form of a serpent and deceived her into disobeying God. Adam followed her, and they did what satan told them to do instead of obeying God. When he (Adam) did that, he made satan his lord. Adam did not take the authority given to him by the Creator over the enemy; he made satan the illegitimate ruler of the earth.

It's encouraging to know that the Power Jesus' Blood has provided everything we need to live a life of victory, including redemption, fellowship, healing, protection, and authority over the enemy. Believers, we must be resolved that this power runs deep, and all that we need is within each of us. Even more important, how many of us use it and apply it in our lives every day? **Selah.**

God is love, and the greatest expression of His love toward us is the Blood of Jesus. That love covers every need man has had or ever will have, and every time we apply the blood, we experience an outpouring of this love. Through the blood, this love has created a barrier between us and all the devil's works.

Through cultivating moral virtues and practicing them, one develops their good moral character. A person becomes who they are by what they do repeatedly and habitually. You create a second nature filled with generosity, compassion, and loyalty. As a righteous person, you are someone for whom the greatest joy is possible.

The contrary holds as well. Someone who repeatedly and habitually engages in immoral acts runs the risk of becoming a bad person. In some cases, one's character can become so brutal or corrupted that they reach a point where rehabilitation of their nature is not possible.

"You're not struck. You're just committed to certain patterns of behavior because they helped you in the past. Now those behaviors have become harmful than helpful. The reason why you can't move forward is because you keep applying an old formula to a new level in your life. Change the formula to get a different result." ~ Emily Maroutian.

133

The Bible teaches that a person can reject the gospel to a point where God in turn rejects them and curses their conscience to sin; having a reprobate mind.

Romans 1:18-20—NIV:

"The wrath of God is being revealed from heaven against all godlessness and wickedness of people, who suppress the truth by their wickedness, since what may be known about God is plain to them, because God has made it plain to them. For since the creation of the world God's invisible qualities—his eternal power and divine nature—have been clearly seen, being understood from what has been made, so that people are without excuse."

Be willing to hear and accept the truth, then use the strength you gained from the truth. Your achievements will be the total of your thoughts. Be more than just a believer; be a real follower of Christ not only in word but in Deed and Truth.

We need to see God's love with miracles, signs, and wonders that Jesus Himself did working through us as believers. Do you have a personal relationship with Jesus as it ought to be, or have desires and tangles hinder you? How far are you today, compared to where you were in your understanding of God's Word a year ago? Understanding the Word is a vital part of strengthening and maintaining your relationship with Jesus.

However, we must not keep what we learn to ourselves; we are to share it with others. We are good citizens, thus good influences and light to those around us in our community. A

river feeds and nurtures it, so showing gratitude and appreciation to your loved ones nourishes your relationships. Let them know how important and dear they are to you and how much better your life is for having them close.

Many people complain that their relationship is failing because they lack communication; we don't communicate. Listen, you send a message every moment when you are in the presence of someone; perhaps you aren't speaking because you are busy doing something else.

If your words don't communicate through your voice your body does. And when you speak, the tone of your voice says more than your words. Jesus left a legacy of obedience and even He did not seek glory for Himself, but to glorify the Father. —**John 17:1-8—paraphrased.**

"I have glorified you on the earth. I have finished the work which you have given me to do. And now, O Father, glorify me together withy, with the glory which I had with you before the world was. "I have manifested your name to the men whom you have given me out of the world. They were yours, you gave them to me, and they have kept your word. Now they have known that all things which you have given me are from you. For I have given to them the words which you have given me; and they have received them and have known surely that I came forth from you; and they have believed that you sent me."

I cannot do anything by myself, but I can focus my obedience to tell others about Christ, and they choose to live for Him. Jesus is still revealing the Father to those whom the Father has given Him, now through us, and we can leave a legacy of glory as we influence others through our lives. Are

you an active member of a local church? Each member of a local church (believers) impacts the other members who comprise a local church.

Please do all you can to ensure that your impact is positive, not hindering its local work. Will you be missed for becoming everything God has put inside to give and share in this world for His good? We can quantify what we do, like how many pages or books we wrote, or how many books we sold.

Being is harder to quantify and measure like being a great Dad, being a spiritual leader, being a compassionate friend, an understanding neighbor, or a caring, loving spouse. Difficult experiences in life often teach us a lot of wisdom. The insights we learn about God, ourselves, and the world can be priceless to those around us as they face their trials.

God does not measure time; He measures growth. The Bible has a lot to say about being an overcomer. Overcomers are followers of Christ who successfully resist the power and temptation of the world's system. An overcomer is not sinless but holds fast to faith in Christ until the end.

The Bible teaches believers to recognize that the world is a battleground, not a playground. God does not leave us defenseless. **Ephesians 6:11–17** describes the armor of the Lord available to all believers. Sometimes all it takes to overcome temptation is to stand firm and refuse to be dragged into it. **James 4:7b—KJV** says, *"... Resist the devil and he will flee from you."*

We do not turn away when times get difficult or become a renegade. Overcoming requires complete dependence upon God for direction, purpose, fulfillment, and strength to follow His plan for our lives. No, people are not what you think because we are so much more!

You cannot fully understand what it's like to be another or their experiences because they are uniquely different. All you can do is have empathy or the wherewithal of understanding another person's thoughts, feelings, and condition from their point of view, rather than from one's own. Sometimes, there are people that you can't help.

There are people in my life that I can't help. To be helped, a person must first ask for help. A person must make themselves available, vulnerable, open, and humble. Second, for you to help someone with your words, that person must first resonate with the kind of wisdom you have to share. Timing is so important; you must be ready for advancement, prepared for growth, eager for truth, hunger for new ways of seeing beyond your limited old perspective. See yourself as loved by God no matter what you have done or what is going on in your life.

Jesus knew and accepted His mission, but what would have happened to humankind if He was not the ultimate sacrifice? Through practicing to listen while spending time with God, can we genuinely know His intent for our lives to be filled with purpose and joy. Cultivate your relationship with God without trying to figure out your life on your own. Let the Holy Spirit reign over your life by being obedient to His reign.

I believed if I gave you enough information to erupt your thoughts, you would quite possibly go after the truth. There is always more in you; you can be better than you were yesterday. For the benefit of all, are you more than what you have become? Admittedly, we are so much more than what anyone thinks as we rise above our fears and doubts to self–awareness into purpose.

Value yourself because you are indeed an expression by the Spirit of God. Come with the mindset of love and impartiality. We will finally see people for who they truly are and not their labels, exterior appearances or first impressions.

Acknowledgement

Thank you, Apostle Purdue, for your obedience to the Voice of God to prophesy His heart that this book was inside of me.

To my son, Isaiah, Thank You for the back-cover photo.

To my daughter, Christine, Thank You for your editorial contribution to the Introduction.

To my Bible study group and specific co-workers, Thank You for your assistance in my research.

Special thanks to my random researchers' who wish to be anonymous for their opinion input contribution.

Thankful for Pinterest for their writer's informational guide.

Writing this book was a humbling learning experience for me, and I pray this is the same for you.

About the Author

Kareen Nelson was born in St. Andrews, Jamaica West Indies, and raised in Mt. Vernon, NY. She currently resides in Fort Lauderdale, Florida with her husband (also a published author) and their two adult children. Kareen is a woman of faith and known for her prophetic wisdom and insight. She is a people person and uses her prophetic gift and wisdom to inspire and encourage as she interacts with people of all faith and background. Kareen has influenced many to choose a life of faith, and how to effectively merge family, faith and business into a dynamic calling.

Kareen uses her degree in finance, her given analytical bent, attention to details, critical thinking, and decision-making skills in dealing with everyone from all walks of life. Her calling and desire is to help as many people as she can to identify and understand how their thoughts, abilities and potential are linked together to guide them to discover their purpose and destiny.

A Different Perspective

www.ingramcontent.com/pod-product-compliance
Lightning Source LLC
LaVergne TN
LVHW051243080426
835513LV00016B/1718